Over the Rainbow
The Love, Loss, & Legacy of Your Dog

"I loved it! Even though it was a difficult subject, I found it refreshing and positive. Losing a pet is certainly a different experience for everyone, and I found Krista covered many different ways to go through grief."
—Josée Ouellette, owner of a Heart Dog

"Krista expertly merges the worlds of storytelling of her own and other dog-owners experiences along with the incorporation of therapeutic techniques and theories. This book is a must-read for any dog-lover who will experience their own joyful pup going over the rainbow at some point or another."
—Hannah O'Reilly, MA, RP

"Recommending Over the Rainbow is easy. Reading about the wonderful dogs that have touched their owners' lives and the grief that can overwhelm them when they lost their friend was cathartic. I smiled, felt reflective, cried a bit and then transitioned to remembering how beautiful my dogs were. Read the book, do the exercises, use the workbook, it will truly help you honor that sweet four-legged friend you've lost by leading you from grief to treasuring your memories."
—Grace Douglas, Heart Dog owner

"I laughed, I cried, I learned, and I felt comforted by the personal stories and experiences shared. The author's heartfelt exploration of grief and loss really resonated with me. The blend of emotional anecdotes, psychological insight, practical advice and opportunities for self-reflection offered me a new perspective on handling grief. This book has not only provided solace but has also equipped me with valuable tools to navigate any future losses. Over the Rainbow is a must-read for anyone who loves their pets and wants to better understand and cope with the emotional journey of loss."
—Eve Maria, cat-owner and High School Resource Teacher

"Krista is a therapist who truly 'gets it' when it comes to grieving the loss of a pet. She reinforces that it is okay to feel your various emotions such as despair, anger, and guilt. She offers various techniques to help one cope and move forward. One can grieve the loss of a pet as one would a human, and at times even more so. It is okay to reach out for help and support if the loss is just too much for one to bear."
—Anda Pember, canine lover and owner

Over the Rainbow
The Love, Loss, & Legacy of Your Dog

Krista Helman, MSW

FernAura Press
Ottawa, ON

Publisher - FernAura Press
101-2039 Robertson Road
Ottawa, Ontario, K2M 1P2

Over the Rainbow: The Love, Loss, & Legacy of Your Dog -
ISBN - Paperback: 978-1-0688463-4-2
ISBN - eBook: 978-1-0688463-2-8
ISBN - Audiobook: 978-1-0688463-3-5

Production Manager: Krista Helman
Cover Design by: Krista Helman
Guided Meditations Narrated and Recorded by: Trina Brunk

In Memory of Aura, Banana, and Bailey.
Thank you for shining light on the little things in life.
I look forward to meeting you again—over the rainbow.

TABLE OF CONTENTS

FOREWORD

I am deeply grateful to Krista for inviting me to write the foreword for this truly remarkable book. I've had the privilege of working with Krista where we provide consultation and train mental health clinicians in EMDR (Eye-Movement Desensitization and Reprocessing). EMDR is an evidence-based modality, effective for treating post-traumatic stress disorder (PTSD), anxiety, depression, and grief.

Krista is an expert in this therapeutic modality and I have seen firsthand how she effectively integrates EMDR therapy for grief. Her heartfelt approach helps people honor their unique journey through loss. There is no one better than Krista to blend her professional expertise with her personal experiences into this powerful book. When I listen to her teach, it feels like I am attending a TED Talk—captivating, moving, and inspiring! I am thrilled that you're about to begin this journey with Krista, as her words will guide you through the grief of losing your dog and help you honor the legacy they left behind.

As a psychologist, I witness in my practice the profound connections we form with our beloved dogs—how they create safety, foster connection, and leave lasting legacies. This bond can be as strong as, and sometimes stronger, than any human we may connect with. We call our dogs "our best friends" for a reason. So, when they die, it can leave a large void in our lives with emotions that feel difficult to overcome. Krista captures this beautifully in her book, offering insight and compassion for those navigating the heartbreak of losing a cherished companion.

In *Over the Rainbow: The Love, Loss & Legacy of Your Dog*, Krista explores significant topics such as trauma, the relationship between trauma and grief, and the impact of grief, specific to our beloved dogs. She presents these complex ideas in an easy-to-understand manner, weaving her clinical expertise with personal narratives. You will learn about Krista's own experiences with her dogs, past and present, revealing how love, loss, and their legacies intertwine.

Prepare for an emotional journey. I cannot promise you won't shed tears, and it's completely okay if you do. Krista's warm, compassionate presence shines through, making it feel as if she is right beside you as you navigate each chapter. Her "Turn Within" moments encourage reflection on your grief, while her "Self-Care Moments" provide guided activities, such as meditations and mindfulness practices. These activities are thoughtfully curated to help anchor you during this process and offer a much-needed respite.

Krista's writing has profoundly impacted my own grief over the recent loss of my dog, Tess. Tess was our family dog and not solely one person's companion. When I moved out to start my own family, Tess stayed with my parents and sister. In late 2022, Tess contracted lymphoma and began her chemotherapy journey. The treatment allowed her to continue to be herself for 10 more months and then her health began to significantly decline. My mother and sister courageously and compassionately decided to euthanize Tess at the end of 2023. Initially, I distanced myself from my grief, internally saying, "Oh, my sister's and mother's dog passed." Even after her passing, I gave mementos to my sister and mother to help them remember her but avoided looking at my own feelings. I did not accept the grief and even questioned if I deserved to feel upset about Tess.

This book taught me that this was okay—that I could experience my grief at my own pace and that I am allowed to feel her loss. Krista's "Self-Care Moments" felt like a warm blanket during these challenging times.

Disenfranchised grief is when the passing of our dogs can be overlooked and is often unacknowledged by society as "real grief". Reading about this concept hit me with a wave of unexpected emotions because it validated my love and connection with Tess and allowed me to see that my feelings were authentic. This book provided me a safe space to reconnect with my memories of Tess and truly mourn her passing.

The book also features vignettes from individuals who have bravely shared their stories of love, loss, and the lasting impact their dogs have had on their lives. These accounts foster a sense of connection, reminding you that you are not alone in your grieving process. Krista has even interviewed veterinarians, providing valuable insights into supporting families through the difficult process of saying goodbye.

As you engage with Krista's activities, she discusses the profound growth that can emerge from grieving and the unique ways we can learn to live with the love and sadness of our departed dogs. She instills hope by explaining the neuroscience behind our grief, assuring us that moving through this process can lead to renewed connection, meaning, and joy in our lives while honoring our beloved companions. Krista poignantly highlights that the depth of our grief reflects the strength of our love, reminding us that the two are inextricably linked.

Krista has created a work that transcends a mere narrative on losing a dog; this transformative book delves into grief, loss, and the enduring legacies of our cherished companions. It is a testament to healing, optimism, and the possibility of renewed life and hope. I am thrilled that you are about to read this book and take this important step in your grieving process because your feelings and your dog truly matter.

Kyle Poon, Registered Psychologist
EMDR Certified Therapist & Approved Consultant
Creator of the YouTube Channel - Calm with Kyle
https://www.youtube.com/@CalmwithKyle/videos

INTRODUCTION

Spring Sunbathing

Our family had a delightful way of knowing when spring finally graced us with its arrival. It was a simple yet heartwarming sight when our pug, Aura, found her way to her favourite spot on the patio. There, she would stretch out, embracing the sun's warmth. Despite her black fur absorbing a considerable amount of heat, it was a heavenly experience for her. She adored those sun-soaked moments!

I will always hold dear to me how Aura taught me the importance of being present. Whether it be a piece of fruit or a laundry basket, she always found joy in the simplest of things, and in each moment as it unfolded. Her outlook on life is part of her legacy, and has forever impacted my existence. Today, I feel privileged and grateful to have loved and lost a dog.

A Message for You

If you are reading this book, you are likely experiencing or anticipating the passing of a loved companion. You may also be someone who is seeking to support someone who is grieving such as loss.

For those who are grieving, I want to send you my deepest condolences. This must be so hard for you. Your dog was more than just an animal. They were a source of connection, purpose, and a friend. Your pain reflects the depth of your love and your connection with your dog.

Even though I have lost a special dog, I still can't know what it feels like to be you right now. That's because everyone's experience with grief is unique, yet none of us can escape it. As I write this, I'm imagining that you are in a dark place, feeling lost and lonely, and I want you know that I'm right here next to you. I won't tell you that your feelings are wrong or that you need to forget your dog. I will sit with you here, for as long as you need.

When my dog Aura crossed over the rainbow, she was ready—I was not. I wish I'd had this book to help me, and so I hope it will help you. Know that it is possible to cherish the memory of your dog without feeling consumed by grief.

What to Expect

Over the Rainbow: The Love, Loss, & Legacy of Your Dog explains the roots of grief and why the loss of a dog hurts as much as it does. The intention of this book is to offer insight and guidance through the darkness of grief.

I invited others to contribute their stories, and that's when I realized so many of us have had the privilege of loving, and being loved by a dog. I was given permission to share personal details of their stories and photos. My personal stories are from my memory, so I did my best to maintain the true essence of my experiences.

You might be wondering why this book includes stories of others. After all, you are reading this book because of your loss, right? The reality is that we need others to move through grief; we cannot do it alone. Although everyone's grief is unique, it can be helpful to see ourselves in the stories of others. Also, by hearing another's story of love and loss, we help keep their connection alive.

Over the Rainbow explores the science behind our very human experience, so your book journey will oscillate between your heart and mind throughout.

I invite you to reflect on your own journey. Together, we will stay in the darkness until you find your way into a new, sunny world. Notice, once again, that you are not alone. We see you; we support you, and we validate your pain. I promise you that one day, you will be able to remember your dog while feeling connected and full. Your grief is a gift, and you cannot benefit from its potential transformation until you first give it time and space, and welcome it for tea. There is no one big thing that can be done to address grief, and time is not the only ingredient.

I invite you to explore and participate in what is offered in *Over the Rainbow*. Although not required to benefit from this book, I recommend using a journal to complete the *Turning Within* questions, and to complete the *Self-Care Moment* activities at your own pace. Recorded guided meditations and digital versions of selected *Self-Care Moments* can be accessed by scanning the QR Codes found in each section.

A workbook intended for grief in general called *Self-Care Moments A Workbook to Navigate Your Grief* is available for purchase at KristaHelman.com. This printed book includes all *Over the Rainbow Self-Care Moments* as well as more practical activities, exercises, and guided meditations.

Why This Title?

There is a written piece called Rainbow Bridge, you may have heard it before. It describes a paradise where pets go after death and wait to be reunited with their owners one day. Although there are multiple versions floating around, the poem describes a lush meadow called Rainbow Bridge, located just before Heaven, where pets are restored to perfect health and happiness, and there is unlimited food and fresh water. The pets still remember and miss their owner whom they left behind on earth, but keep busy playing and frolicking together all day in the sun until their owners join them. When the owner dies and is on their journey to the afterlife, they make a stop at Rainbow Bridge. At this point, the pet stops playing and then looks at their owner in the distance. The pet eagerly runs as fast as they can to their owner, and they cross Rainbow Bridge united as they go into Heaven.

Multiple claims have been made as to the original author. In February 2023, *National Geographic* published that it was originally written by Edna Clyne-Rekhy in 1959, as a way to cope with the loss of her dog Major. They quoted the entire piece, and here is a small portion of what was declared as the original version:

They all run and play together, but the day comes when one suddenly stops and looks into the distance. His bright eyes are shining, his body shakes. Suddenly he begins to run from the herd, rushing over the grass, his legs carrying him faster and faster, and when you and your special friend finally meet, you cuddle in a happy hug never to be apart again…

This is not a religious or spiritual book; but our journey dips into the reality of after-death communication researched by science, and the healing value of this phenomenon. In the final chapter I'll explain more, but I really had no choice but to write this book. If I hadn't completed this book, I assure you I would have been haunted for the rest of my life! I asked the Universe for guidance, and even though I did not like the answer I received, I have to concede that the Universe is always right.

The title of this book, *Over the Rainbow: The Love, Loss, & Legacy of Your Dog*, was chosen as a reference to the poem Rainbow Bridge. It captures the universal emotional journey of pet loss, and acknowledges the grief of our furry friends. It reinforces the idea that love transcends death. Many of us wish for a reunion in a beautiful afterlife, and it resonates with the themes of love, loss, and legacy explored in this book. My message to you is that our relationship with our dog mattered.

Overview of Grief

Grief comes in many shapes and forms. It can result from a major life transition, death of a loved one, a relationship ending, or reality not matching the dream. Whether the trigger is death, divorce, losing a job, a child leaving home, illness, retirement, miscarriage, when we lose someone or something dear to us, our whole world shifts without our consent. We are forced to adapt.

We instinctively sense a separation, frequently accompanied by strong emotions. Attachment patterns are set in childhood, so experiencing a loss can stir up memories and feelings of past grief, making it even harder to cope. This can result in trauma, where our emotional pain blocks the ability to access important happy memories.

Experiencing grief is uncomfortable; moreover, many of us have been socialized to believe that it is unacceptable to express the emotions that come with grief. That's why in the past we may have shied away from others, and we might be experiencing this from others now.

The loss of a dog can be equally if not more painful than the loss of a human. Yet, for some reason, society often sends us signals that it's unacceptable for us to mourn our loss openly. The pain we experienced since our dog died may have been overlooked, leaving us feeling unseen and alone in our grief. The pain is real because the connection and love is real.

Self-Care Moment: In Preparation for this Journey

For most people, love is the most profound source of pleasure in our lives, while the loss of those whom we love is their most profound source of pain. Hence, love and loss are two sides of the same coin. We cannot have one without risking the other.
- Colin Parkes, Love and Loss: The Roots of Grief and Its Complications

I want to start with an obvious statement: *Over the Rainbow* is about the grief and loss of your dog, that special creature that came into your life, and knows you like no other—that forever faithful companion who was always near your side. Specific examples in this book may activate your grief and loss of a human loved one, of your pet, or of another loss. This can happen unexpectedly, and that's ok! Let's be prepared.

Take a moment right now to ground yourself in your surroundings. Notice the sensation of your feet on the floor and the support of your chair against your back. Look around you, noticing what's to your left, and to your right, even glancing up at the ceiling and down at the floor to sense the boundaries of the room. Take note of any windows or doors nearby, reminding yourself that you're in a safe space.

Your well-being is important, and I cannot emphasize this enough: if you are getting activated, please practice self-care. Take a break, go for a walk, listen to a meditation, or contact a support person.

List some of your favourite grounding tools. You can use slow, deep breaths: In for 4 seconds, out for 4 seconds, and repeat 4 times. Another option is in for 4 and all the way out for 8.

If you need support while reading this book, list who you can contact. (visualize that person now)

CHAPTER ONE: *THE LOVE*

The Story of Aura

In 2013, I was thirty-five and living the life of a single mom with three young children. I juggled multiple jobs, served on a board of directors as a volunteer, and worked toward finally completing my university degree full-time. Every day brought phone calls from the school about my child's behaviour, numerous doctor appointments to manage, and the feeling of not belonging among my university peers. I struggled to balance soccer, school deadlines, and dinner. I felt confident while writing papers about the social and structural challenges of the upcoming Silver Tsunami of baby boomers in healthcare, but then I would find myself in tears after struggling to explain basic long division to my child. My ex-husband and I, as parents to our children, did our best to co-parent, but each interaction left me feeling overwhelmed with a sinking and racing heart.

Let's hit the pause button for a sec so I can give you a little insight into my life at that time. My parents could share many stories of me growing up and how I tested their parenting. As a child, I struggled to sit still throughout school, struggled to read the room, and constantly made famously impulsive decisions and poor choices. Living in a neurodivergent body was not an available explanation at the time. As a result of experiencing a childhood full of constant correction and redirection from parents, peers, and teachers, it started to take a toll on my self-esteem. I had spent my adult days trying to prove to my parents that I could finally make sensible decisions, you know, as one often does.

At the time of our pause in this story, I wondered if I was making more messes than the usual parent. I even questioned my new career path as a social worker, thinking that maybe I had too much baggage to handle other people's feelings. And to top it all off, there was a new guy in my life who was treating me like a queen, and I had no idea why. Looking back, it was as if I had some sort of programming blocking me from reading his signals of kindness and acceptance. I felt like I was doing a dance in quicksand with an audience waiting for me to sink—again!

I often questioned whether the challenging behaviours my kids were displaying stemmed from their own undiagnosed trauma or if I was simply too overwhelmed in my new reality to distinguish between causes and effects. I was unsure if I was contributing to my difficulties, or if external factors were at play. Outwardly, I projected confidence with my mantra, "Failure is not an option," but inside, I was dealing with numerous losses. My marriage ending shattered my dream life, and I grieved for my children becoming "children of divorce," something I never wanted. I also had to adjust to a new financial reality, including selling my fancy dining room set to make ends meet.

My children were content with the new plastic folding table and chairs, feeling well cared for and secure in my home. However, inside, I was walking a tightrope over Niagara Falls, juggling responsibilities and uncertainties. I knew they relied on me to stay balanced and strong, but I questioned how I would navigate our challenges and reach safety. I had to find a way to get everything right.

I started exercising and meditating regularly, and this brought me much-needed clarity. When the kids were visiting their father, I missed them, but it also gave me the silence to reorient my life and prioritize what truly mattered and what I needed. This reflection led me to a profound realization: adding a dog to our lives would play a significant role in our healing journey.

Adding Calm to Chaos

The woman on the phone explained that she was downsizing due to a divorce and had to rehome many of her dogs and cats. Because of my divorce, I was searching for a furry companion for myself, and hopefully, a soothing best friend for my children.

I wasn't sure what to expect as I drove up to the old, dilapidated farmhouse. The doorbell did not work, but within seconds, the chorus of dogs barking was enough to announce my presence. The woman introduced me to her many dogs, none of them being the dog I had spoken to her about. She interviewed me in great detail, explaining that the pug I hoped to adopt preferred cats and spent most of her time sleeping and playing with her cat siblings. I explained that I'm allergic to cats, so I didn't have any, but I could offer this dog a home of constant snuggles and attention. After more interrogation, the woman put the other dogs away and said she would get the dog I was waiting to meet. I wondered if there had been an issue with this dog getting along with other dogs. *Was I about to meet and bring home a damaged and dangerous dog to my children?* I began to wonder if I should leave.

The woman came back with a shiny black pug. The dog was three years old but still very tiny. Immediately, the dog jumped on my lap and insisted I pet her. I instinctively rubbed her chest as she melted into my arms. We had just met, but I felt a familiar connection with this animal. I asked the woman a few more questions, then turned to the warm bundle of fur in my lap and asked, "What do you think? Want to come home with me?" Aura started to lick my face excitedly and hugged her paws around me. That was it; a bond was made. She chose me as a friend and connection for life.

I knew the children would be excited to welcome a puppy to

our home, so I surprised them with the arrival of Aura. When they got home from school, they bleated with joy and rolled on the floor with her. They were over the moon!

On the surface, I know it may have looked like I was adding chaos to chaos by adopting a dog, but Aura proved to be one of the best decisions of my life. She was a warm, comforting hug for my kids during those tough early days after the separation. Always there with a wagging tail and a listening ear, she became their loyal buddy, offering a safe haven from the ups and downs of adjusting to new routines. My kids often shared how much they appreciated her company, especially after a long day, and they needed comfort and fun. They'd spend hours playing dress-up with her, hosting tea parties, and creating imaginative adventures together.

Aura never judged me; she saw me as perfect. She didn't mind when I was too tired to cook and got the kids McDonald's again or when I had a pajama day and left the laundry unfolded. Every day, she showed me unconditional love, accepting me just as I am. The only "flaw" she might have seen in me was that I didn't always share my food with her. She didn't focus on my failures, gossip, or keep score. She was an important safety in my world and, in addition to my children, a reason to keep going. When I wanted to curl up into a ball and make the world go away, she seemed to know that was the time to shove her yucky ducky stuffy in my face, or to meld her warm body next to mine.

When the kids weren't around, Aura was also always by my side, whether I was in the backyard or the bathroom. She loved being near me, dozing off in her favourite spots: the cozy laundry basket or the sunny patio stones. It was clear she adored soaking up the sunshine during her peaceful naps.

Aura's serene presence was a welcome relief. While outwardly, I projected strength and composure, when the children were away, I faced the abyss of loneliness. In those moments of heartache, Aura was there, bringing a smile to my face, offering comfort with her gentle snuggles or a playful pug snort. She had a unique ability to absorb negativity, living up to her name with a mystical touch. Her intuitive companionship made me feel understood and valued when I needed it most.

It's not always true that you have to love yourself before you can possibly love another; I was very capable of loving almost everyone but myself. Aura became my guide on the journey to rediscover self-love, a path I needed to traverse before fully welcoming a new partner into my life. While my boyfriend, now my husband, was incredibly supportive, Aura's presence was pivotal in helping me reach a place where I could fully embrace the love he offered. Eventually, my husband and I blended families, and I gained two more children and two more dogs. All felt wonderful, for a while.

Turn Within: What did your dog teach you about yourself?

Self-Care Moment: Self-Care Menu

It's important to do something compassionate for ourselves every day. Write a list of at least ten things that you can do as a form of self-care. Perhaps it is being curled up in a blanket drinking your favourite tea, listening to uplifting music, exercising, resting, having lunch with a friend, or making a healthy meal. Other self-care activities that can nourish your mind, body, and soul include meditation, time in nature, or practicing gratitude.

Keep this list as a menu to refer to when you notice you need it. Pick one thing from this list—and do it now!

Scan the QR code to complete this Self-Care Moment:

Understanding Grief

We can understand the experience of grief through the stories of others, but there is also value in learning about the science behind this universal human experience.

The terms grief, loss, mourning, and bereavement are often used interchangeably, but each carries a distinct meaning. Loss refers to the experience of being separated from someone or something significant. Grief is the emotional response to that loss—the inner experience of feelings such as sadness, anger, guilt, or longing. Mourning is the outward expression of grief. Bereavement refers specifically to the period of intense grief and mourning following a death-related loss. Over time, we often learn to carry grief in new ways, and its intensity may change, but the impact of the loss and our connection to it can remain throughout life.

Human nature is to connect and attach. We feel loss when someone or something we cherish is no longer attainable, or as we desire it to be. This can make us feel powerless. It's not how we could categorize the relationship that matters; it's the separation from the bond and shared memories that causes us to experience grief. The stronger the bond, the more painful the separation. There is no way of escaping it! Grief can result from much more than death: loss of safety, trust, and significant relationships of all kinds. It can be realizing that our life is not as fulfilling as we wish.

Breakups are a common source of grief. In extreme cases, particularly in younger people, this can lead to suicide out of hopelessness. This happens because with limited experience in the world, it can feel impossible to imagine a future beyond the relationship. It can feel like their whole world is shutting down. The person they identified as being closest to is no longer available, and their brain needs time to adjust. It is a challenge when they still see that other person on social media or in the classroom. The fact that they still physically exist but are no longer available for connection is extremely confusing and painful.

Not feeling seen, heard, or valued as a child creates a loss in the form of attachment injuries. Traumatic moments such as COVID-19 created loss where many of us experienced a loss of freedom, stability, predictability, and connection. Even positive life milestones can also create unexpected loss, such as a child leaving the house for university, life after retirement, or starting a new job. These are just a few examples of where loss can enter our lives.

We can also experience anticipatory grief, where we know death is certain or near. An example of this is when we see the decline in the health of someone we love. It can be hard for us to absorb reality when we cannot control things we wish we could; sometimes bad things happen, and some things can't be fixed.

Grief is the internal emotional response to a perceived loss including emptiness, anxiety, anger, guilt, and a longing to be with. At our core, under all the emotions of grief, is sadness and a desire to recover what has been lost. We can also experience conflicting feelings: relief and sadness, excitement and isolation, peace and regret.

As there is no escape from loss, there is also no escape from grief. Grief is a natural reaction, and if we don't allow ourself to feel, we can get stuck. This is common where there is an underlying issue such as trauma. Grief can be considered a form of traumatic loss, as it takes a significant amount energy for us to avoid, navigate, and process it. Although grief evolves over time, it never fully goes away. It usually comes and goes in intensity, as milestones and celebrations reactivate our feelings again and again. Generally, with time, painful thoughts and memories will transform into moments of re-experiencing connection.

Mourning, on the other hand, is how we express our grief to the world while we are adapting to our new reality. It is how we cope and is reflected in our feelings as well as how we relate to the outside world. These public and private displays of grief can be conscious or unconscious. This can look like crying, wearing black, or staying curled up in a blanket. All feelings of grief are acceptable, but not all expressions of mourning are healthy. We might distract ourselves by overworking, overeating, increased use of medication, or binge-watching TV. Mourning can also involve avoiding and numbing through consuming drugs or alcohol, or other self-harm. We should try and mourn in ways that allow us to feel the full feelings of grief, but that are safe for our mind and our body. Cultural practices and rituals can influence and support our mourning and help guide us through our grief journey. Mourning is necessary as it assists us to adjust to the changes in our new world as a result of our loss.

Bereavement is the period of time when we experience grief or express mourning. It is the process of reorienting and adapting to life without the deceased. We need time for this to happen.

During this period, there will be good days where we are managing well and feeling positive , as well as sad days where we want to avoid everything and everyone. It's really common to be high functioning at work, then collapse and feel very sad at night. This doesn't mean we forgot our loved one during the day; it means we were able to contain our grief for a short period of time. Although it can be helpful to contain our grief when needed to function, it is also draining! We do not want to contain our grief all the time, as we need to feel it in order for it to transform.

Grief and mourning do not follow a straight line. The only rule is we must feel it to get through it. While we may grieve forever, the intensity of our emotions usually lessens over time. Most of us will feel the full effects of our loss around six to nine months after it happens, but it is also perfectly normal to take two years before the full extent of the loss is felt. Grief in and of itself is not a mental health condition or a disease, but it can become one if we get stuck in processing our grief.

Our brain has to accept that our loved one is no longer with us, and we must allow ourselves to feel our feelings. Navigating grief involves a specific kind of brain flexibility called neuroplasticity. As we reorient and remap the connections in our brain and body, how comfortable we are with facing and feeling our emotions is an important factor in how we process grief. Our mental and physical states are especially critical during the time of our loss, and can influence how manageable our journey through grief is.

Sometimes, we may look to things like alcohol, new relationships, or work to help ourselves feel better during bereavement. While this may feel like a helpful coping strategy at first, in the long run it may hinder our grieving process. Avoiding our feelings or finding distractions can make it harder for our brain to adjust to the changes around us. No one is in denial of their loss; they are in a state of being unable to accept, accommodate, and assimilate for their loss. In the absence of movement and growth through grief, we may repeat our choices and patterns, or become physically ill. Grief recovery includes acquiring coping strategies that we never have been taught, and finding meaning within our relationships.

It can be helpful to imagine grief beyond just sadness and see it as a state of motivation. While sadness is part of it, grief is like a strong desire, such as really wanting a drink of water on a hot day but not knowing where to find one. If only we had a kitchen sink in front of us, complete with running water and a clean glass. As we find ourselves suddenly in the middle of a desert of grief, we can long for an oasis of fresh water somewhere, but we have no idea which direction to take. Our brain keeps thinking about how we used to get water from the kitchen, but the only option we have is just to start walking in search of water. Only when we find the oasis do we gain new mapping information for our brain to accommodate for our new reality. Updating our mind map and knowing where the oasis is in space and time fulfills our need for water.

Studies using brain scans show that grief activates parts of our brain that drive motivation and seeking. This core feeling of longing is linked to dopamine, a brain chemical known to be related to desire and reward. Knowing this helps us see that grief motivates us with anticipation and action. It's not just about feeling sad; we are actively seeking what we have lost and have no concept of how to get it or feel connected to it again. The powerful yearning that grief sparks make us search for our loved one while at the same time, literally causing us pain. From this we can understand that even after our loss, our brain keeps expecting our dog to be there. Understandably, we do not like experiencing an intense yearning for something that we cannot fulfill and have no direction to get it!

Some studies have shown that higher levels of hormones in our body, like oxytocin, can make grief feel more intense. There is also lots of evidence explaining that when we experience grief, our brain remembers other past losses that we have not resolved, making a current loss feel even bigger.

Everyone's physical body and lived experience are different, and it's normal for people to move through grief at different speeds. The key is to understand and accept our feelings without trying to push them away. This understanding helps us navigate grief with self-compassion and acceptance.

Grief is something that everyone goes through at some point. How deeply we feel it and for how long also depends on how close we are to the person or thing we've lost, our attachment patterns, our physical and mental health and how well we are able to manage the feelings and emotions that are part of the journey of processing the separation and reattaching to memories.

Hearing about the passing of a dog we encountered regularly at the neighbourhood dog park can be really sad, especially if they seemed happy and healthy just a short while ago. But this will not match the grief we feel with the passing of our dog, our best friend. A significant loss can change how we see life, turning things that used to make us happy into sources of sadness. While we will always wish our dog was here, the sadness will fade as we journey through grief and prepare to thrive in a world where someone important will always be missing. .

Turn Within: Have you been turning to unhealthy or unhelpful coping strategies?

Why it Hurts So Much!

Aura loved sleeping on the sunny patio, and after she died, her special spot made me sad. On many sunny days, I sat in her spot and cried. I knew she was gone, but a part of me hoped that if I just sat there long enough and wished for her to be there, she would somehow manifest in my arms. I even rested my face against the patio, hoping I could feel her again. My heart area ached. I had thoughts that were not true, such as that I had killed her, and that she felt I had betrayed her. Logically, I knew these thoughts were ridiculous and that she was never going to show up, and I questioned why I couldn't just let her go peacefully. I have since discovered that my brain was not interested in the truth, and there was no amount of talking that would have convinced me otherwise. I have also learned that it makes sense that it hurts so much when we lose someone we love. To be human is hard; it means we must connect, and that means, we have to feel.

From a young age, we naturally form strong bonds with a few important people in our lives. This bond, called attachment, is all about feeling safe and secure. We instinctively attach to our caregivers in the hope they will keep us alive and provide food, shelter, and comfort. The people and pets we attach to also act as a mirror, shaping the stories we tell ourselves about who we are, and the world around us. Attachments help us to form our identity. We automatically want to stay close to who we attach to, and so, how they respond to our emotional needs, especially during times of stress, shapes our attachment patterns. The way that we attach in our early connections defines how we try to attach to our other relationships throughout life.

When someone we love dies, it feels like the bond we had with them is broken because they're no longer with us physically. Loss can impact our sense of comfort, security, meaning, and balance in life. The world we once knew and could predict has changed without our consent, leading to a loss of what our brain assumed was true and stable. When our mind perceives a threat to our safety and security, our attachment system reacts accordingly, even if the threat is not real. This activation of our attachment system can lead us to cry, seek attention, or do whatever it takes to remain close to the loss.

When these attachment bonds are threatened or broken, it's natural to feel intense anxiety and deep emotional pain, regardless of whether those relationships are positive or negative, secure or insecure, peaceful or full of conflict. This is because when we experience loss, our world changes drastically, and things will never be the same. Our brain takes time to adjust to our new reality. Parts of our world that we used to know and predict no longer exist because what we are attached to, our dog, is no longer with us.

Understanding how our early attachment experiences shape our coping mechanisms in grief today, can be helpful to understand ourselves. A secure attachment from childhood gives us a lasting sense of value and support throughout our lives, which continues to guide us through future losses. Because of this, people with secure attachments often find it easier to adjust and progress through the grieving process. Sometimes in childhood, the person we attach to as our source of safety can also be a source of fear or terror, and this can contribute to a disorganized/insecure attachment pattern. If we learned to shut down emotionally or deny our own needs as a child because our caregiver was unpredictable, dangerous, or neglectful, we might struggle to cope with grief and have more intense reactions to loss.

Attachment is crucial for survival and is hardwired into our brain. It's essential to understand that attachment isn't the same as love. Love encompasses the safety and security of attachment plus a deeper emotional connection. Even in challenging situations like abusive environments, children can still form attachments to their caregivers. Attachment is an instinctual mechanism that secures the relationships necessary for our survival as infants.

Not all attachments are as life and death as when we are young. We can also develop an attachment to other people, animals, or things. We still feel grief even if we weren't deeply bonded with what we lost, and this is why grief is not straightforward!

The intense pain we feel when we lose someone or something we're attached to is rooted in our instinct to maintain the connection, something we learned from our childhood attachment experiences. As human beings, we resonate with these extreme states. This is why many songs are about heartache and loss, or about love and joy. We are drawn to and bond through shared intensity. The attachment style we develop as a child influences our future reactions to loss, and the more we depend on what we lose, the harder the loss can feel.

When our dog's eyes met ours, and we received the message from them, "I love you, you are perfect, and I'm so glad that you are mine!" our brains encoded a deep bond that can exceed that with a human.

Looking back, I depended on Aura as a constant source of safety in my world during a very difficult time of my life. Even though I was in a great place in life when she died, a constant physical cue of security was suddenly gone. At the most basic level, this was terrifying for me.

Turn Within: How has your special bond influenced your grief?

Vagal Tone

When life becomes overwhelming and grief weighs heavily on our hearts, our bodies often react by going into survival mode. Some of us are more familiar with this state, especially those who naturally tend to feel stressed or anxious in everyday situations.

But there's something fascinating that can help us navigate these tough times—our breath and the amazing vagus nerve. The vagus nerve is the main nerve of our parasympathetic nervous system, and part of our autonomic nervous system (ANS). It is a superhighway of information and action in our bodies that helps control things like how fast our heart beats, how we breathe, and even how our stomach works. Think of an orchestra conductor telling our body what to do and how loudly to play the music, without us even thinking about it! The vagus nerve plays a crucial role in how we respond to a threat. It helps maintain social engagement, calmness, and a sense of connection with others. This is our default state when we feel safe.

When we take slow, deep breaths, we activate the vagus nerve in a way that tells our body it's okay to relax. It's like a gentle reminder that we can let go of some of the tension we're carrying inside, and it helps us to access the attachment and connection we still have with our dog. Especially when we release deep breaths all the way out, our heart rate tends to decrease. This is helpful because deep exhalation activates our parasympathetic nervous system, which is responsible for calming the body. As a result, our heart rate slows down, helping us feel more relaxed and centered. This can be incredibly comforting, especially when we're going through a challenging time like grief.

When we practice deep breaths, we are improving our vagal tone; how strong and healthy our superhighway of information operates. Having strong vagal tone helps us feel calm, happy, and less stressed. This can be a powerful tool. It's like controlling the conductor of an orchestra so we can adjust the volume of the music. This protects and directs us from feeling too sad or upset. So, when we do exercises like focusing on our breath, this helps us self-regulate, feel more connected, and build resilience in our bodies.

There are many breathing techniques to strengthen our vagal tone. My favourites are the breathing exercise at the beginning of this book and Colour Breathing at the end of this chapter.

Dr. Porges is a researcher who is known for developing the Polyvagal Theory. This theory explains that our internal sense of safety or danger affects our capacity to effectively interpret our environment and our needs. He developed a therapeutic approach called the Safe and Sound Protocol (SSP), which uses sound and frequency to access and work with the vagus nerve. I use SSP regularly in my practice to help my clients regulate the volume of their orchestra before we start trauma work. People love it because all they have to do is relax over multiple sessions while listening to music. I know it sounds too good to be true, but I have seen the extreme benefits with many people. Once the orchestra volume is adjusted, it is much easier to deal with trauma and stressors.

Meditation, yoga, exercise, massage, and cold-water immersion can all strengthen vagal tone. Making sounds with vibrations such as singing, gargling, or humming have also been shown to help.

Feeling more calm is not forgetting our feelings or pretending everything is okay. Instead, it's about giving ourselves a moment of peace and finding strength within us. As we practice breathing exercises, we'll likely notice several benefits as we activate our body's parasympathetic nervous system and counteract the stress response. We may experience better management of our emotions, and feel more relaxed as our stress hormones regulate. We may also notice improved focus, a quieter mind, and feeling more grounded.

Velociraptor in the Forest

Andrew Huberman is a neuroscientist and professor at Stanford University. He's dedicated his career to research and practical education, making the complex world of neuroscience accessible to many. He states, "You cannot control the mind with the mind." With this, he is referring to the autonomic nervous system (ANS), which governs our basic functioning and more. Our ANS connects to all organs in the body and is a two-way street of information and activity. Our vagus nerve is the part of the ANS that helps us feel calm.

In the name of survival, when we are distressed, our ANS keeps us ruminating on our upsetting feelings and circumstances. Whether we experience emotional or physical fear, stress, or anxiety, all involve high levels of alertness and awareness. Our body wants us to remember the threat so that we can be on alert and protect ourselves! In this state, time seems to slow down. We might even be noticing this right now—feeling as if grief will go on forever. Interestingly, when we are in happy states, time seems to go by faster. In happy and calm states we tend to accept that our circumstances of happiness could end at any moment.

It might be helpful to also understand how our body deals with stress. Imagine we are walking in a Jurassic forest, and we suddenly hear leaves move and twigs break. It might be a Velociraptor dinosaur about to jump out, so our ANS hijacks us! Our heart rate quickens and energy is mainly focused on our bigger muscles so that we can prepare to make quick and big movements as needed. We might see our hands shake uncontrollably. Our energy is redirected away from our reproductive and digestive organs because they are not needed for a survival response. Our pupils dilate to take in more light, which narrows our vision. This means we cannot see things well in our periphery, but we gain precision in assessing what we are focusing on. Our thinking is ignited, and as we hone in on the direction of the potential Velociraptor, our mind is lightning quick assessing: *If this then…if that then…* When we realize the noise was just a mouse rustling in the leaves, our body usually goes back to a rested state, called ventral vagal.

The deeper and longer we enter a survival response, or, the more Velociraptors we perceive in our environment, the harder it is for us to bring ourselves back to a ventral vagal state. We need to find a way to slightly lower the volume of our ANS response so that we can gain more control, shift our perception of time, and enjoy the present. We can use the body instead of a cognitive approach. Activities that strengthen our vagal tone and reduce our heart rate include mindful meditation, breath work, and social connection. These can help us relax and return to a more regulated ANS pattern. We can also use therapeutic imaginal exposure to confront our fears. Kyle Poon, Psychologist and the author of the foreword for this book has an engaging YouTube channel that I often refer my clients to for mental health related exercises.

What we perceive as a potential Velociraptor threat depends on what our forebrain has decided is threatening. We may become hypervigilant or numb to a potential threat as a result of trauma, or we can desensitize ourself to threat through exposure. The difference is choice. For me, just thinking of my daughter rock climbing gets my ANS activated! When my daughter chose to learn how to rock climb, she did so at her pace and continued to choose to do it again and again. If she were in a safety harness and fell from a high height, this could be traumatizing the first time it happened. The next time she was in a safety harness, she'd likely have an ANS response in preparation for survival. This is because trauma adjusts our ANS programming so that we are prepared to respond to a threat next time. This reprogramming is helpful when there are Velociraptors, but can work against our best interests when we are in a safe and secure environment.

Even if we chose euthanasia out of love, the death of our pet was still not our choice. If we had the choice, they would still be here with us alive and healthy. The grieving process can feel like a Velociraptor, but it isn't.

As we will learn more throughout this book, the emotional pain that comes with grief is helpful. It is what motivates our brain to remap the connection we have with our loved one, so that we can feel connected again.

Although the circumstances surrounding a loss can be traumatic at times, at its core, grief is simply an ANS state of sadness and yearning, because we don't know how to connect anymore. Grief's process is about restructuring our internal map of where our dog is and when we will see them again. We are motivated and have a desire to reconnect to our dog in space and time. As we move through grief, we experience a gradual decline in this motivation, and gain a new concept of our dog. When this happens there is no more autonomic arousal, and we finally sense peace and connection.

How to Move Forward?

The first step into the storm of grief is actualizing the loss. The best way to move in this direction is by talking about our loss. Journalling or talking to someone about how the death happened, how and when we learned about it, our experience at the celebration of life, and what others said about our loved one are all areas to explore. Externalizing our experience instead of running it as a loop in our mind is key. Talking and externalizing helps us come to grips with the reality of the death. Visiting or touching something tangible reminds us they are gone. This can be the gravesite, something they wore often, or a photo. If we have hesitation, we can question what our fantasies or fears are about doing these things. We can also verbalize, draw, or journal current and past memories of our dog.

The next helpful approach is to accept that the waves of grief are pain with a purpose, and that we will get through it. Feelings like anger, guilt, loneliness, anxiety, and sadness are all uncomfortable but necessary aspects of the grieving process.

Adapting to our loss also requires us to learn to live without our dog and make decisions. Knowing what new problems have entered our lives after their passing can prepare us for this change. It is also helpful to reflect on our moments of mastery, to remind us that we already have all that we need inside us.

What Not to Do

It's common to become fixated on the cause of death, but this is distracting from our movement through grief. Understandably, we may have thoughts of seeking revenge or justice if the death was due to the mistreatment of our dog. Although this can be helpful in preventing the person from doing this again to someone else, spending our life focusing on pursuing a lawsuit will not likely make us feel better, and it certainly won't help us move through grief. We would not miss them any less if they died in a less painful or violent way. Grief already takes up a lot of our energy. Consider if feeling whole and connected again is a better focus. Doing so will make us a better advocate in the future, as our actions will not be guided solely by emotion.

Another common mistake we make is blaming ourselves and saying we feel guilty. Guilt suggests we've done something with the intent and motivation to harm. I do not believe we had the intent or motivation to do harm. Instead, I believe we are feeling sad, and as a society, we seem to have lost what that core emotion of sadness feels and looks like. It's understandable that we wished things ended differently, so instead, let's accept what we wish we did more of, differently, or better. This is a more helpful approach.

We may have been told that time heals all wounds. Sometimes, wounds need stitches or get infected; we may need extra or immediate action. We can learn that we have more control than we initially thought. If the loss has not happened yet, we can prepare for grief, and if the loss has already occurred, we can embrace the journey for all it has to offer. What we choose to do over time influences how we move through grief.

We may also have been told to be strong for others during past times of loss. This strategy does not make sense for our loss, because it does not help us deal with our own grief. Sometimes, keeping busy is what was modelled for us in terms of how to deal with grief. It is important to remember that keeping busy is a distraction from feeling our feelings, a key component to moving through grief. To move through, we must discover and experience all feelings involved, as well as take steps to adapt to our new world.

We may also have been told to ignore what we are feeling and that we are responsible for others' feelings. We may have heard, "Stop your crying; you have no reason to cry right now!" or, "You think _____ and _____ when really you are _____," or "There you go, turn that frown upside down!" These messages suggest we have to control our feelings for others and shut down what is happening inside us. If we learn this as a pattern, we start to lack something called interoception. Interoception is the ability to be aware of what our internal sensations are telling us. This can include our heart rate, hunger, respiration, temperature, physical pain, and our emotions. If we don't make changes, we can start to feel like a victim. We are not helpless; we can take charge of our internal change.

Trying to numb or distract our pain with food, alcohol, anger, sex, exercise, isolation, fantasy, drugs, or retail therapy is also not helpful. All loss consumes an immense amount of energy, and engaging in these other activities can be exhausting and harmful if doing so in the extreme. We may feel a temporary relief, but we can end up feeling remorse and shame, which adds to the weight of grief. Also, when we bottle-up our feelings instead of feeling and releasing them, we can start to feel a sense of desperation for relief, leading to an emotional explosion or impulsive behaviours that we regret. The activities in this book are designed to act as a release valve to release the pressure in a more productive way.

Feel, but don't flood! A common theme throughout this book is that we need to acknowledge and feel all our emotions and the consequences of the loss in order for our minds to remap to our new reality. It is not helpful if our emotions flood us to the point where we cannot care for ourselves, putting us in harm's way. There are many options available to us, such as practicing containment techniques or speaking with bereavement specialists and support groups; please reach out to one if needed.

We are not defective because we are feeling sad. Reading this book means we are open to finding a new way to exist. Many of us were never taught how to grieve, and the messages and models we get from society are mixed. Undoing some of what we've previously learned is part of this journey.

Finally, we should avoid making any major life-changing decisions during the early phase of bereavement, and while experiencing intense grief and mourning. This means not moving or selling our home, or adopting a new pet in order to avoid feeling the feelings. We are likely best equipped to deal with grief while in a familiar environment and with as little stress as possible. We want to avoid introducing a sense of helplessness, and want to promote resilience.

A Bond with a Dog

Aura had anxiety when crated, so she quickly earned our trust to have full access to the house all the time. Every night, my husband and I would go to sleep with a firm rule: no dogs in the bed. Like clockwork, at 4 a.m., I'd be slightly woken as Aura quietly snuggled up next to my feet. She knew to stay on my side and to be quick about it, as my husband would have put her back on the floor—only for her to jump up again on my side once he fell asleep again! She preferred chicken over beef, sun over rain, and enjoyed car rides. Aura loved to hunt for sky raisins. She didn't mind getting her nails done and *loved* to greet me with a wet snort on my face. My attachment system programmed Aura as a sense of comfort, safety, and acceptance in the world.

When we discuss a caregiver's attachment to a child, it involves providing care and comfort to the child. On the other hand, a child's attachment to a caregiver centers around feeling safe and secure. We all need to feel seen, heard, and valued. Throughout life we are programmed to welcome attachment opportunities that meet these criteria.

A bond with a dog is a perfect fit because they are actually experts in the areas of attachment and love. We depend on them for safety and security, and they offer us unconditional acceptance. Some of us even feel safer being vulnerable with a dog than with a human!

Dogs have made headlines with heroic life-saving stories, such as saving children from drowning and protecting us from intruders. Our dogs can encompass various roles, from being a partner, a child, and a friend. We provided care for them, and at times, they cared for us. This suggests that our attachment to them spans across a spectrum of attachment categories, making it even harder for us to process our grief. This is why it hurts and why the pain is so excruciating. You'll always miss your dog because you'll always love them deeply. That strong bond creates a lasting connection, which is how attachment operates.

Sometimes, a bond is slower, such as with a rescue dog, where trust is earned, then connection follows. Many people say their connection with their dog is more than love; it's almost as if there was a reunification when they first met. The relationship can feel symbiotic and fulfilling. Whether the bond is instant or an evolution, when a dog has bonded with you, you know you are experiencing something special.

Dogs are renowned for their joyful welcomes at the door, their love for cuddles and physical affection, and their adorable puppy dog eyes that melt our hearts. Think about the COVID-19 lockdowns and all the cute dog videos that boosted our mood! Dogs seem able to read our needs and can be loyal to a fault. Dogs have found ways to connect deeply with us. The grief we experience from losing a dog is just as profound as grieving a human loss. It is no surprise to me that we invited them into our camps and our families a long time ago!

The loss of a canine friend can be devastating because you did not lose a something; you lost a someone. When your dog died, your attachment system got activated with many of the same reactions as if you were in childhood, being disconnected from a caregiver. Your system has perceived your attachment bond as severed because your dog is no longer physically here.

They Can Save Our Life

I was delivering a presentation to a group of fellow therapists. At the end of my presentation, I showed a slide with my contact information and an image of the cover of this book. As I explained that I was writing a book on the grief and loss of a dog, most people in the room automatically responded with a singsong, "Aw." This happened again, such as when I shared the news with my bi-weekly networking group of entrepreneurs, and also when a stranger overheard me share about my dogs and my book. It was clear to me that their pets had profoundly influenced their lives and, at times, even rescued them. Again and again, simply mentioning the topic of my book would elicit a heartfelt reaction, with people placing their hands on their chests and eagerly sharing their personal stories of love and loss.

The loss of a furry friend can mean the loss of many things. Perhaps they were our only friend, our support for anxiety, our healthcare companion, or our sense of safety and protection. Dogs gladly fulfill these roles in our lives, whether as guide dogs for the visually impaired, companions for those with autism, sources of comfort for those battling depression, or simply as emotional support. The possibilities seem endless.

The bond with a pet should never be underestimated. In my early days as a social worker, I was stationed at a downtown community centre doing outreach. People were invited to come and get support and get out of the cold to enjoy a warm cup of coffee. There, they could experience a brief break from the hardness of living with homelessness. One day, a man came in who was keeping to himself in the corner. His hood was up over his head, and he seemed to be really enjoying his warm coffee. I went over to introduce myself and I noticed something moving around his neck in his hoodie! He saw my surprise, and he looked down to the floor. He apologized and started to walk out the door. Before he could leave, I smiled at him and asked what was in his sweater. His eyes perked up as he explained that he had found an injured rat, nursed it back to health, and formed a friendship with it. His new friend found a home in his warm sweater. The man shared that his choice to keep his pet rat meant not being allowed to sleep in the shelter. He explained that his rat was special to him, and the only soul he trusted. His pet rat was his reason to stay alive.

A bond is a bond. While you might not want a rat in your sweater, your connection with your dog is yours to keep; no one can take it, and it will never be forgotten. To be seen and valued through the eyes of another is a gift. If you take a moment to remember how your dog made you feel seen and valued, I bet you'll also notice the gifts they gave you. That happy wagging tail at the door, they were happy to see you. Now take a moment right now, and see if you can put yourself in their paws. Feel the joy they felt when you reached down to say hello back. Notice the moment when you made them feel seen and valued. Our relationship with our dog is a two-way street. They bonded with us just as much as we bonded with them.

The Story of Lua: Coping with Grief

Lua, a Nova Scotia Duck Tolling Retriever (Toller), held extraordinary significance in her owner's life for many reasons. Lua was adopted when her owner was 17, and served as a lifeline amidst her owner's mental health struggles. She also offered companionship in a home where one parent travelled and moved frequently for work, and another parent was often occupied as the primary caregiver of her grandmother and other siblings. When Lua joined the family, her owner's mental health was very low, and basic daily tasks were a challenge, such as getting out of bed, eating, showering, and going to school.

The daily routines and needs of a dog served as anchors for Lua's owner, encouraging her to regain a sense of responsibility and structure in her life. Playful interactions and quiet moments of companionship with Lua became essential elements that motivated her owner to reestablish stability. Also, daily walks increased the likelihood of socializing with others, and allowed Lua's owner to develop meaningful connections and friendships with other Toller owners. These new relationships, alongside Lua's quick intelligence, evolved into adventures in competing in in rally-obedience as well as agility, and in therapy dog training. Lua was titled and recognized as the #4 Toller in Canada, and eventually participated in field competition.

Beyond the titles and formal recognition, participating in these activities gave Lua's owner the opportunity to get out of the house, explore new interests, and develop the courage to try new things. This sense of normalcy contributed to her owner's overall well-being and mental health. Through Lua's eyes, her owner found herself drawn out of isolation, engaging more with the world and rediscovering the simple pleasures of everyday life.

Lua was also present for her owner through multiple abusive relationships, the deaths of family members and loved ones, challenges completing her university degree, as well as other health complications and life transitions. Through all that, Lua was a consistent source of unconditional love, always sitting close by or putting her head on her owner's lap. This invited Lua's owner to hug her and cry into her fur, and go for long walks regardless of the weather. She felt accepted and seen without judgment by Lua. Lua's intuitive nature seemed to sense her owner's needs. For all these reasons, Lua's owner is eternally grateful.

After two days of minimal eating and a thorough assessment with the veterinarian, Lua was diagnosed with cancer. The vet suspected the cancer was in her spleen and liver, and spreading quickly. Lua would only have another week to live without chemotherapy and other invasive treatments, which may only have extended her life by a few months at most. This news was shocking and devastating, especially because other than the recently decreased food intake, there were no behavioural changes or evidence that Lua was sick. Also, Lua was still young regarding her breed's life expectancy, and she had recently passed her annual check-up with no sign of illness or abnormality.

After much thought, reflection, and deliberation with family members, Lua's owner opted out of medical treatments. Instead, pain management and palliative care was chosen for the remainder of Lua's life. Her owner was fortunate to have an understanding employer who allowed her to take time off work. During this time, Lua was taken to her favourite walking paths, was offered her preferred food and treats (including ice cream), and had organized visits with her favourite people and dog friends.

Lua's behaviours and symptoms at nighttime became increasingly difficult. She was constantly whimpering and pacing, unable to get comfortable or settled. At that point, her owner recognized that Lua was declining quickly and arranged for a vet to come to the house to carry out euthanasia. As Lua ran out of time on this earth she was blessed by a local minister, and a comfortable space was provided for her to rest at home. Despite the difficulty of this decision, it offered her owner reassurance that Lua would avoid experiencing significant pain and discomfort in her final moments.

When the day of the vet appointment arrived, it seemed as though Lua had an intuitive understanding of what was to come. She chose to lie down in the main hallway of the house, where she could observe everyone moving about. Her owner carefully carried her to her favourite room, which was adorned with cushions, blankets, and mementos that captured their time together. Upon their arrival, the vet took the time to introduce themself and explain the procedure of euthanasia. She assured Lua's owner that there was no rush, allowing the family the space they needed to say goodbye. The vet's compassionate gesture of offering a candle and a personalized rock with Lua's name provided a sense of comfort and ongoing connection.

As the procedure commenced, Lua's owner stayed by her side, expressing love and gratitude for their time together. Lua died in her owner's arms, a sensory memory that forever became etched in her owner's mind. The family took several moments petting and hugging Lua's deceased body as they said their final goodbyes. Her dignified and heartfelt farewell concluded with the vet wrapping Lua in a soft blanket, and offering assistance as her owner carried Lua's body outside.

After the vet left with Lua's body, the owner collapsed to the floor and cried for several minutes. She held onto the pillow Lua rested on, and eventually fell asleep where Lua had peacefully passed away.

During the following days, Lua's owner confirmed the

cremation details and purchased Lua's paw print, which was pressed into a clay mold. This and a few other items, such as Lua's collar and leash, are still displayed in her honour today. A small pouch of Lua's fur is kept by her owner's bedside, which her owner occasionally takes out to touch from time to time. Lua's pillow is kept nearby as an object to sleep with or as support in her owner's chair, serving as a reminder to pause and think of Lua, and then attend to the feelings that come up with her memory. Her owner also makes a point to talk about Lua, recalling memories of her with family and friends.

Several things eased the grief of Lua's owner. Most notable was having people around her with whom she could talk about her thoughts and feelings, including her partner, friends, family members, and therapist. Having safe spaces like this allowed her to get her feelings out rather than suppress them. She notified people in advance so they would be prepared to support her and so they could also prepare for their loss. Friends and co-workers made a point to visit Lua's owner. Some gave flowers or plants, while others offered to take her out for coffee or a walk. These check-ins were found to be helpful, especially when others offered space to talk about her thoughts and feelings rather than trying to offer advice. Taking measures to honour Lua has also helped.

Lua's owner is grateful to have had knowledge of Lua's illness in advance so she could prepare for her loss. This also granted her the ability to be intentional about how they spent time together in Lua's final days. She was also fortunate enough to be working for an employer with a deep understanding and compassion for people experiencing loss, even regarding pets, and she realizes this support is not something that everyone can experience.

From time to time, Lua's owner states she can still feel the sensation of Lua dying in her arms. While she finds this feeling extremely difficult and haunting, she does not regret choosing to have Lua in her arms for her final moments.

Lua's owner would like others to understand that sometimes,

grief related to the loss of a pet can be even more challenging than losing a person in one's life, and she wishes society would recognize this more often. The inability of others to relate to our experience is what makes grief so difficult and isolating, regardless of similarities in experience or the time that passes. Lua's owner feels that if she did not have a support network, then she would have sought a pet bereavement group offered through the humane society or a community group. Grief related to the loss of a pet is valid, and the capacity to cope with it can grow over time.

Turn Within: What was helpful for you when your dog passed?

What is a Heart Dog?

One day, my student asked me about my current dogs. It was a moment of personal connection, where once again, dogs played a role in bridging that gap. I shared stories about my three dogs, highlighting their unique personalities and how they each bring something special into my life.

Hero is a stray dog breed called a Potcake, and he was rescued from The Bahamas. He got his name because he was found on the street protecting a younger litter of pups from traffic. He is the smartest dog I've ever met. He has the most majestic mane of fur, which blows in the wind as he looks at his reflection in our pool— and he chooses to do this often! He also likes to ask to go outside in the winter, just so he can sit in the snow and watch us inside as if we are on television.

Nilla, our French Bulldog, is the most dramatic soul I've ever met. If she is upset with you, and she is never hard to upset, she will literally make a scene by storming to the other side of the room and turning her back to you. No eye contact—well, maybe a little side-eye, as she wants to make sure you are noticing her. She is also a crabby boss queen in general, and we work on her tolerance of others every day. With her garden variety of health issues, she always has aches and pains and unless you are in her good books she is simply a miserable dog. Think of the character "Red" from the Netflix show *Orange is the New Black*. One of Nilla's favourite things to do is to hold a chipmunk stuffy in her mouth while she kicks a small tennis ball, as if she's playing soccer.

At roughly twelve pounds, Lemon is a petite princess pug who refuses to exit the house unless the weather is perfectly sunny and warm. She repeatedly expresses this preference by relieving herself on the kitchen mat instead of our large backyard. She insists that she is the cutest, most deserving of all the animal kingdom. Lemon loves to snuggle under the blankets, completely covered! Like my human children, I love my fur babies equally, yet differently. Aura died before we adopted Lemon, and if she were here, I know she would have taken Lemon under her wing just like she did with all the other dogs who came through our home!

My student then shared about her dog and asked, "What about past dogs? Have you ever had a very special dog?" I was caught off guard and, in my most professional voice, shared with her about Aura. "Ooh, you had a Heart Dog!" she said, "I had one too and still miss her very much. Isn't a Heart Dog just the most wonderful feeling?" After having many awesome foster and resident dogs come through my life, I can agree that Aura was extra special, and definitely was a Heart Dog!

Heart Dogs are more than just lovable companions; they represent a special bond that transcends the ordinary. If you're reading this, chances are you've experienced the unique connection of a Heart Dog in your life. A Heart Dog isn't just a pet; it's a soulful companion that leaves a lasting legacy of love and life lessons. This term encompasses a profound and evolving relationship where both owner and dog shape each other's lives in meaningful ways. The bond with a Heart Dog is incomparable, characterized by a strong connection and a unique depth of love. Sometimes, we realize we have a Heart Dog from the start, while other times, it's only after they've crossed over the rainbow that we fully grasp their significance. It's even possible to have multiple Heart Dog relationships throughout our lives.

A love experienced with a Heart Dog is not superior to that felt with other dogs; it's just a different colour of love. If you haven't felt this special bond, remember that your relationship with your dog is unique to you, and only you can define its significance. No matter what words you use to describe your connection, you get to keep it forever.

Turn Within: Journal a description of each of your dogs. Are any identified as a Heart Dog?

Grief is the Price We Pay

At one time, I felt that life was cruel and unfair because a dog can bring so much joy yet does not live as long as we do. I opened my heart only to inevitably experience such intense pain! I wondered why I did it and why I knew I would do it again.

Grief is the price we pay for the love we have for our dog. It is a result of the profound bond we share with them, and this is a natural human experience. Grief represents the emotional volume of love we invested in them. Loving our pets means we will likely one day experience loss with their death. The pain of separation from our dog triggers a deep primal response within us, and this is because our bond with them is real and strong. Research has shown that the same parts of our brain react to emotional pain as they do to physical pain. So, when we grieve, it's not just in our heads—it's a real feeling and physical sensation rooted in attachment.

Pain is usually a signal to our body and mind to try and learn from our experiences, so they do not happen again, and grief does not feel good. Our bodies are designed to react to emotional experiences to protect us and to help us learn how to survive in the future. When we grieve and yearn for their return, it is our body's way of telling us that something we love has been lost, and this feeling might be a threat to our survival. Our bodies do not like to feel a lack of control, and unfortunately, our minds often struggle with accepting things we can't change, like the loss of our loved one.

Grief can be confusing and make us feel powerless. We might find ourselves replaying the story of our dog's life and death over and over as we try to make sense of it. In everyday problem-solving, reliving and questioning our decisions and how we got to that point can be very helpful for us to learn and grow. However, this is not as helpful when there is powerlessness in the situation, because no matter how many times we replay the movie, we can't change it, and we can't stop it from happening again.

We struggle to process what we cannot control, and we will all be confronted with grief at some point. We can't avoid loss, and some things simply can't be fixed. Loss is a universal experience, and grief is a natural part of life. But until we go through it ourselves, we might not fully understand how difficult it can be.

We can try to avoid the feelings of our grief, but if we do this, our grief will get in the way of us fully feeling the love and connection in our relationships for the rest of our lives. By embracing our grief and honouring the love we shared with our dog, we acknowledge the depth of our connection with them.

Grief is a testament to the joy and companionship our dog brought into our lives. When we face our grief and acknowledge gifts from the time we had with them, we grow.

When clients talk about losing their dogs in therapy, they often share their pain, cry, and then say "sorry" as they try to pack up their feelings. What they might not realize is that I understand the depth of their sorrow because I've loved a dog too. I believe dogs reflect the best of who we can be, and it seems absurd that society makes us feel we have to apologize for our grief. Dogs help show us the best of ourselves and help heal our troubled parts. It shouldn't be strange to feel grief for them!

I've cherished all my dogs, each one shaping my life. Aura was special in a way that's hard to explain; her love was a different kind of brightness. If grief is the price we pay for the gift of having a dog in our lives, then grief is something we should embrace instead of pushing it away. Love never dies, and when grief is transformed—and we find a new way to exist and feel their love in their absence—we evolve and grow.

It's okay to let go of our pain. I promise we will never forget them, and we will always keep our love for them.

Pain is not required long-term for this transformation; remembering their legacy is. I'll always love and wish Aura was here. Acknowledging this, I know my grief won't completely go away. Today, when I think about her, I feel a gentle ache in my heart, and then it quickly turns into a warm smile inside.

Self-Care Moment: Colour Breathing

This activity is a guided meditation to increase a sense of relaxation and peace. Meditation can be helpful for grief as it can help us with emotional regulation, stress reduction, and self-reflection.

Colour Breathing can be adjusted to suit your needs. You can bring in a colour to help you feel energized or motivated, or perhaps, a colour for self-forgiveness. You decide. Some people find it helpful to either wear their colour of choice or have this colour in their workspace to help cue them to colour breathe often.

Listen to the guided meditation here:

CHAPTER TWO: *A GOOD DEATH*

The Story of Aura: Cats & Foster Dogs

When Aura was about seven years old, a family member took care of her while we were on vacation. There were two resident cats in the home—and my understanding was that Aura loved cats. I thought, what could possibly go wrong? Apparently, Aura was curious about one of the cats and they did not appreciate her attempts to make friends. The cat swatted at Aura to keep away, and her eye was scratched. Bulgy pug eyes are prone to injuries, so we went through the usual protocol with a specialist to help her heal. Unfortunately, after many months and many dollars, her eye was not getting better, and we could tell she was in pain. We made the decision to have her eye removed, and about a week after the surgery, she was like a puppy again!

I know that some people questioned my decision to save her eye with the expensive eye surgery, but for me, the decision was not even a question to consider. If we did not do the surgery, she was in pain. If we chose euthanasia instead, it would go against my values as a caregiver. She was only seven years old, and I felt she was deserving of a longer life without pain. Aura had thoughts, needs, and feelings. She was not just another piece of furniture, she was my dog, a companion, a best friend.

As the kids grew up, we decided to open our home to foster dogs. I felt like this was a way to instill my social work values in them, and they loved welcoming and saying goodbye to each new foster. Aura was an exceptional co-host to over fifteen foster dogs. She taught them where to find food and where to go potty. She guided some in learning manners and reassured others about safety and belonging in our pack. Confident yet gentle, Aura helped the foster dogs adjust to their new reality. Despite her preference for cats, Aura excelled as the ultimate foster dog host, and became the respected matriarch of our dog family.

As Long as You Know You Are Loved

One day, when Aura was around age nine, I noticed she was not in the room with me, or sleeping in the sun. I found her in the TV room, staring at the corner of the room. "There you are!" I said, and she came running for snuggles.

Over the next year and a half, her brain tumour and doggie dementia progressed. The barking would reliably begin around 10 p.m. and then increase with frequency and intensity. As the moments of her getting lost in a corner became the norm, I'd find her, and we'd celebrate, joking that she found me. Even though the vet said her tumour was not treatable, I convinced myself she was not sick. So I'd let her sleep peacefully most of the day, hoping she rested enough for a few lucid hours together after dinner.

Eventually, she was in the same space as me less than 20 percent of the time. She started to spend her few waking hours barking relentlessly in a room alone, or roaming the halls aimlessly and afraid. It was as if she'd suddenly lose her vision. She's have no sense of who we were, then all would return to normal for a very short time. Each time she'd "go" I'd grieve her absence, and each time she'd "come back" I grieved because I knew it would not last. We had to start crating her at night because she was disturbing everyone's sleep by wandering the halls and barking all night. Looking back, I think she was very confused and afraid. I guess I couldn't accept what that would mean.

One evening, I was lying on the floor next to her dog bed when she finally woke up. Her tail wagged, and she kissed my face. As she started to fade, I pleaded for her to stay. I started to cry. "I promise to keep you here safe and cared for, as long as you are somehow aware you are loved!"

As days passed, Aura's symptoms continued to increase in severity and frequency. During her last summer with us, she kept walking into the swimming pool. We tried to protect her. Adding a garden fence only worked temporarily, so we'd take turns watching her when we'd let her out in the backyard. Even with these precautions, I still had to jump in the pool and pull her to the surface just in time on many occasions. She didn't even try to swim.

Her inability to understand and navigate her surroundings was becoming a constant. My love no longer consoled her. Instead, my touch made her twitch and back away.

Because I Love You, It's Time

In the late winter of 2021 Nilla was about six months old, and was entertaining us with her energetic 10 p.m. zoomies. She was racing from one end of the room to the other, bouncing off the couch and spinning around. As I filmed this insanity, we laughed so hard our stomachs hurt. It was only when I reviewed the video for editing that I noticed Aura's depth of despair. As Nilla's body swept across the screen, the eerie movement of Aura was seen in the background. Aura was walking past the entrance into the hallway, her paws faltering with every step, the sound of our laughter sending tremors of fear throughout her body. It struck me then how oblivious I had been to her distress. She appeared adrift and fearful, disconnected from the warmth and security that she was once familiar with. At that moment, I realized that Aura's time with us was drawing to a close. As spring was near, my husband and I agreed that this would be Aura's last patio season.

That summer, the warmth of the patio seemed to be her only comfort left. Sometimes I would sit next to her, close enough to feel near to her but not so close to startle her. She still had moments of lucidity, but they were few and far between. Winter was coming, and we knew it would not be kind to her. Because of my love for her, I knew it was time to say goodbye.

A friend suggested an organization of veterinarians who

come to your home to perform euthanasia. When the petite and smiling veterinarian arrived, I said to her, "Aura's having a great day so far!" I secretly hoped the vet would permit me to keep Aura a little longer. Instead, the vet offered a soothing look and said, "How wonderful that Aura is able to be here to say goodbye; that happens a lot." I held in my tears and showed her the way to our kitchen, where my husband, five children, and two other dogs sat on the floor in a circle. They were waiting to say their final farewell, as we thought that is what Aura would choose if she could.

Aura ate chicken, one of her favourite foods. We each said our goodbyes with varying intensities. As this was during the COVID-19 pandemic, we all had masks on because we had a visitor in the house. My quiet tears and warm snot were smeared all over my skin behind my mask but in that moment, I didn't care. Aura needed to feel safe and calm; that is what mattered.

The vet administered the medication to make her sleepy. Aura relaxed in my arms, I knew it was my call to make. The vet looked at me, and I gave the final nod to administer the last injection.

As Aura passed away in my arms, I quietly sobbed. I will never forget the exact moment her spirit left her body. I remember her going limp and then feeling lighter. I leaned down and whispered in her ear, "I'm so sorry, I love you so much."

As if on cue, Hero slowly approached us. When he sniffed Aura his eyes bulged wide and he ran to the corner and lay down with his back to us. One of the kids got up and left the room. Another gave me a hug. We all deal with grief differently, and every way is okay.

More tears and snot filled my mask as I cried out loud. As I looked up to see my husband and children also crying, I instantly got angry with myself and thought, *Why did I let COVID and this vet make me wear a mask to say goodbye*! Of course, this was just me trying to make sense of the uncontrollable and very unwelcome shift in my world. Blaming the vet for wearing a mask and for my pain made much more sense at the time than accepting my good friend was actually gone—forever. Her last breath was traumatizing for me; that's why I apologized to her. Part of me thought I had betrayed her.

The vet left quickly after she had offered the option of ordering Aura's ashes, and handed me a few clippings of her fur in a mesh bag with a candle, "Some people prefer to keep a part of their dog to touch," she said. I still have the candle in my living room. I also keep her collar tucked away in a drawer we never use.

As I started to process Aura's passing, I was filled with mixed emotions. I felt at peace, at fault, and relieved all at the same time. I questioned if I was simply selfish to let her go so quickly, then back to feeling selfish for keeping her here so long in terror. Her terror! It kept replaying in my mind.

From time to time since then, I've questioned if I should have tried expensive treatment for Aura or if I should have kept her around longer. Logically, I know neither of those options would have the outcome of her being here today. I've now realized that I had no choice but to make the decision of euthanasia, out of love.

Now when I watch that video of Nilla having a puppy zoomie and Aura wandering in the background, I know that Aura has forgiven me. Perhaps, she even thanks me. I now realize that mask or not, she couldn't see my face anyway. What was important was that Aura could smell and feel me, and sense that she was in loving arms.

When my time comes, I believe Aura will be waiting to greet me. She will be eager to show me her new favourite napping spot—in the sunshine.

A Letter from Grief

Dear Krista,

First, I want to say this must be so hard for you. Aura was a very special dog, and I know the bond you share is deep.

People know me by many names, I've been called Heartache or Sorrow. I am the result of you loving your dog, and my message to you is that your love was worth the pain.

You felt me the other day while in the backyard. You placed your hand on the cold patio stone, and you cried. I weighed heavy on you when you opened the drawer and gently touched Aura's worn and discoloured collar. When the house felt empty as you walked in the door, I did that. That black hole suctioning inward in your chest, that's me. Sometimes Depression, Guilt, and Anger follow me around, but Sadness and Longing are really at the core of my existence.

The pain you feel is normal, and it has a purpose. I see you mourn by numbing yourself. You cannot hide from me or from experiencing your loss. I will still be there when your glass of wine is empty, your bag of chocolate chips is consumed, or when you run out of work. You are only prolonging the pain. You keep hoping I will leave, but I am all your love with no place to go— for now.

Understanding is the first step to freedom from my weight and darkness. There is no shortcut to evolving and adapting to your new world, and I promise you won't always feel this much longing. Today, you must feel everything. When your clouds of pain lift and the sun comes out, you will finally see the path of what to do with all your love.

Sincerely,

Grief

Self-Care Moment: Drawing Grief

Drawing our grief helps us better understand what we feel so we can identify it and work with it in a more helpful way. This exercise is about identifying, feeling, and externalizing your grief. Don't worry about how your drawing looks; go with what you feel!

Listen to the guided meditation here:

Euthanasia

As we shift focus to the very important topic of euthanasia, I should warn you that I have some very strong personal opinions about it. We are all free to our outlooks on certain subjects, and I'm expressing mine here in a general sense. It's possible that I'd challenge something I've written given an unknown circumstance. This is a sensitive subject, so please take care as you read this section.

Euthanasia is kind when there is no other choice. When a puppy eats yet another expensive leather handbag, euthanasia should not be a choice. When a dog is anxious due to past life circumstances or because of human-created situations within their home, and the owner refuses to participate in consistent behaviour training, euthanasia should not be an option. When a dog is adopted, then a baby or two join the family, and it gets to be too much responsibility for the adult humans, euthanasia should not be a consideration. When a loving owner dies and no one in the family is willing to adopt the family pet, euthanasia should not be on the table!

It's pretty clear that I don't agree with convenience or revenge euthanasia. It does not make sense to me that it is considered as a solution because a dog was acting like a dog, life got too busy, we got bored, or no one wanted the pet of a deceased loved one. Instead, I recommend bringing that dog to a rescue so they can enjoy another chance at life. Human convenience or anger should never be a motivation for euthanasia.

However, I approve of euthanasia when it is the right thing to do and is a loving act. It is a kindness in veterinary practice, in that it ends suffering. The School of Medicine at the University of Missouri explains that the name "euthanasia" comes from the Greek words *"eu"* (good) and *"thanatos"* (death). Good Death. The name speaks to the intent of kindness involved so it can relieve an animal of a slow, painful, or undignified death.

I have worked with many people in my therapy practice who

feel responsible for the death of their dog, and it's common for us to tell ourselves that it was our fault so that we don't have to accept the fact that we had no control. This may be because of an accident or because they felt pressured. When we have to make a decision out of love, or on the spot and we aren't ready for it, or the decision is made for us, it is not the same as making this choice out of resentment or convenience!

I fostered dogs and watched many of them go from a terrified, broken soul, to learning to trust and love again. If your dog was a rescue and you had to choose euthanasia, you may have questioned your decision. Remember, you rescued them when you adopted them, and your decision to end their pain rescued them again. The first time was toward trust and love, and then you offered them the gift of peace.

If we chose euthanasia, we may have convinced ourselves that we betrayed someone who showed us constant love and empathy. If we had no choice but to opt for euthanasia out of love, we have to remember that this ended their pain and suffering, and that is one of the most loving things we could have done for someone we loved. Deciding to give our dog peace and sending them away with a soft goodbye is not a betrayal!

Pause to remember how your dog followed you around, greeted you when you got home and looked at you lovingly. Our dogs have no choice but to do those things for us. They had no choice but to wake up from their nap and come see us at the door because they loved us. They had no choice but to lick our tears and make us laugh. That was the power of their love for us.

We had no other choice but euthanasia because of our love for them. Remember, dogs speak in the language of love and kindness, and they would probably do the same for us if they could. They understand our decision.

Sarah Hoggan is a veterinarian whose TEDx talks went viral on the topic of euthanasia and pet loss. Her message of self-compassion in her video is echoed throughout this book:

When your pet is in pain, when they are struggling to move, struggling to breathe, when there is nothing more that can be done, giving them a soft goodbye and sending them peacefully to heaven is a kindness, not a betrayal.

The pain of pet loss is real because the emotions you shared were real. The grief associated with pet loss is valid, because you did not lose a thing; you lost a someone, someone close, and someone special to you. …The dysfunction you suffer after losing a pet isn't just valid, it's normal. Do you know what else is normal when you lose a pet suddenly, or you have to make a euthanasia decision? Reliving every moment and every decision that led to that point. You do that because emotional pain hurts just like physical pain, and we are hardwired to recognize pain as a teacher.

No matter how logical, the decision is not easy. By ending their pain and suffering, we chose their well-being over our needs and desire to keep them here. That is love. We really had no other choice.

We all hoped our dog would pass away peacefully in their sleep, and when euthanasia was performed, this was exactly the experience of our dog.

Claire Place Veterinary Hospice

In October of 2023 I interviewed Dr. Lianna Titcombe, a veterinarian and the founder and owner of Claire Place Veterinary Hospice. She is the International Director of the Companion Animal Euthanasia Training Academy (CAETA), and a regular participant in professional development such as the

International Association for Animal Hospice and Palliative Care Conference. She also offers bereavement training in the veterinary community.

Claire Place Veterinary Hospice is a mobile service in Ontario, Canada, that provides in-home euthanasia and end-of-life support for pets. Their goal is to provide peace and comfort for families and pets during the end-of-life of animal companions, and they support and guide pet owners through the emotional and difficult decision to say goodbye to their animal friends.

This is also the organization that I chose to help me say goodbye to Aura. I have to say, compared to the traditional experience of euthanasia in a standard vet examination room, their services offered my family a beautiful way to say farewell!

As a veterinarian experienced in euthanasia, Dr. Titcombe shared insights on grief and loss from her unique perspective. She recognizes both the emotional weight and the positive impact that euthanasia can have in easing a pet's suffering and ensuring a peaceful passing. Dr. Titcombe is passionate about the importance of dignity in end-of-life care for pets. She navigates this delicate balance by providing compassionate care while respecting clients' wishes. She sees euthanasia as a humane way to relieve suffering, prioritizing the well-being and comfort of pets. She emphasized that while death is a natural part of life, suffering is not acceptable. She believes in relieving suffering, even if it means accepting that death as part of that relief.

Dr. Titcombe discussed the challenges that she sees pet owners face when making end-of-life decisions for their beloved pets, particularly when it comes to euthanasia. She has witnessed how the emotional connection that owners have with their pets can make it difficult for them to choose to end their suffering. She feels it is important to guide her clients who struggle to let go; it's not about an unwillingness to say goodbye, but rather an inability to make that decision alone.

She wants others to know that even she is not immune to this issue. She shared a personal experience of her own struggle with this decision regarding her cat's end-of-life care, and the pivotal role her colleagues provided her in clarifying her decision:

> *I really struggled with my own decision-making, and I needed to look to my colleagues to help me. I had a cat who was beyond ready to pass on. I had him in the clinic, and he was on IV fluids. And I had to read his chart to read what the vets had written. And somebody wrote the word cachectic, which basically means, the body is failing. And I had never looked at him like that. I still wasn't letting go.*
> *I asked the internist to do an ultrasound to see what else can we could do, and he turned to me and said, 'You know, Lea, he's just not a happy cat.' And after that one sentence, I was like, you're so right. He's so not happy. And I let him go that day. But I needed someone else to tell me that. So, it even happens to us. So in talking to clients, I say 'We're going to make this decision together' to take some of the burden off of them.*

She also addressed the common tendency for pet owners to second-guess their decision of euthanasia. She empathized that there's never a good time for euthanasia but rather a right time based on our pet's well-being. Our discussion touched on differing opinions regarding quality of life and suffering:

> *I try to reframe and say, 'You offered the gift of a peaceful passing, rather than subjecting them to a potentially agonizing and drawn-out death…I heard a definition of suffering that I really quite like, which was the idea that suffering is pretty much anything that denies you the expression of your true self. You know the you that you're supposed to be, the life you're supposed to live, and it's been denied for whatever reason. Most people think suffering equals pain.*

This perspective encourages us to consider factors such as loss of mobility, chronic illness, and a diminished experience of life. A deeper understanding of suffering allows us to compassionately navigate the difficult choices involved in end-of-life decisions for our pets.

Throughout the conversation, Dr. Titcombe spoke about the importance of making decisions based on the best interests of our pet, even if it means making a difficult choice. She urged vets to show kindness, and learn to have open talks about a pet's pain to guide owners to make well-informed choices:

Owners don't have the medical knowledge and are so emotionally connected to their pet that it's almost impossible for them to choose to end the life of that beloved pet. The idea is to guide clients who can't let go. It's not that they won't. It's that they can't. They need somebody's help. They need a professional to guide them, to tell them that it is okay to validate their decision.

When caring for a patient who can't fully comprehend, the key is to prioritize their comfort and provide constant reassurance throughout the medical care. She drew a parallel between human end-of-life care and pet care, where minimizing fear, anxiety, and stress for patients and families is important, especially during their final moments:

Usually, there is a moment where they feel weird but don't know why because you can't say to them in words, 'I've given you a sedative, count down from 100, you're going to feel a little sleepy. It's okay, we've got you.' So, we don't have those words, but we have the family try to comfort them, pet them, talk to them while they're asleep. And we try to make it as quick and smooth as possible.

Dr. Titcombe discussed the process of euthanasia for pets, and suggested potential improvements that could be implemented in regular veterinary practice. For example, to ease the pet's anxiety and make the experience less stressful, she suggests that an oral sedative at home before entering the clinic is ideal. She explained the injection process, and how usually in a clinic, an animal has an IV put in before any sedation, which can be stressful.

Emphasizing the need for as little stress as possible, Claire Place Veterinary Hospice meet pets in the comfort of their home, then gives an injection into the muscle as a sedative effect before proceeding. Only when the animal is relaxed is an IV inserted to administer the final anesthetic medicine. This approach may take longer, but it is less stressful for the pet overall. She feels it is important for everyone present to remain calm, to convey a sense of safety and love to the pet as they pass.

She expressed her concerns about limitations and gaps in formal veterinary education regarding euthanasia support. Despite the lack of comprehensive training in this area, she has taken proactive steps to seek additional training and education, and acknowledges that this is not an option for everyone in her field. Her perspective on the lack of professional preparation for end-of-life care and support of families has driven her to offer professional education in this area. In this role, she works with students and professionals to teach the importance of knowing what to say and what not to say:

> *I say, 'All of your patients are going to die, most of them with your help, and only a small handful are going to get Addison's disease or diabetes that you're learning so much about.' I'm still rolling that boulder uphill to try to change the system. But we don't get a lot of training on that, and we certainly don't get training on how to help the people, and especially at the end of life.*

She highlighted the significance of witnessing someone's grief by offering a simple yet effective phrase, "This must be so hard for you." Many people struggle with how to navigate their own grief and often fear saying the wrong thing to others despite good intentions. Dr. Titcombe believes that professionals and a support network can be helpful:

> *The first thing I say is 'One of the best things to say is nothing. Listen. And then, I'm really sorry for your loss.' I think people over-complicate it because they're really afraid of the bereaved, so*

they tend to avoid them, which is the worst thing you can do.

Dr. Titcombe also has extensive experience facilitating pet loss support groups. These spaces offer informal meetings guided by respectful guidelines. This ensures a safe space where individuals can share if they wish, and finally have their emotions acknowledged. She believes in the power of group support, fostering friendships, and sharing experiences to help navigate grief collectively.

She also expressed the importance of seeking professional help on an individual level for those needing additional support, as support groups cannot assist with all types of experiences:

When you try to go out to the park without a dog, people don't know who you are, they kind of look past you, and you've lost a little bit of your identity. So people struggle a lot with that and then they don't want to go out. And then now that affects their mental health.

Overall, the role of Claire Place Veterinary Hospice is one that demands a delicate balance of clinical expertise, emotional intelligence, and a genuine commitment to the well-being of both pets and their human companions. Dr. Titcombe's insights remind us of the need for a compassionate, informed, and supportive approach to pet euthanasia, with a focus on promoting the dignity of pets throughout their end-of-life journey.

The main takeaways from my discussion with Dr. Titcombe were to try and reframe euthanasia as a gift of a peaceful passing, a relief from suffering, and maintaining dignity rather than a negative act. If we can view suffering as something beyond physical pain, we can begin to accept the idea that suffering results from anything that denies the expression of one's true self or quality of life. Informed decision-making is a must regarding euthanasia.

Veterinary professionals can reduce stress and anxiety for all involved when they are able to hold our grief, and offer honest communication. This creates a more peaceful environment during end-of-life times. Professional support should be offered with empathy, acknowledging the emotional burden and trauma associated with our experiences as pet owners.

Capital City Specialty & Emergency Animal Hospital

I also had the opportunity to speak with Brandon Zweerman in October of 2023. At the time, he was the Managing Director of the Capital City Specialty and Emergency Animal Hospital in Ontario, Canada.

I even got a tour of the facility. As a social worker who used to work at a human hospital, I was impressed with what I saw. The hospital boasted state-of-the-art surgical bays, heated floors in the recovery rooms, an ICU unit, and specialized departments like Ophthalmology, Oncology, and Cardiology. One standout feature for me was the bereavement room, which felt like a warm and comforting living room with lots of natural light. It was unlike the typical sterile environment of a veterinary hospital.

Experiencing that it is possible to prioritize compassion and support in a veterinary environment, Brandon has a holistic understanding of pet loss. He noted the difference between human healthcare which often prioritizes prolonging life without considering quality of life, and veterinary care where there are more discussions about quality of life and decision-making:

> In human medical care, our goal is to keep the person alive with the least amount of symptoms. I think in the veterinary world, there are more conversations about quality of life and decisions because it's just a different mindset.

Brandon talked about how euthanasia practices for pets have

evolved over time, with a focus on the emotional impacts. He mentioned that having a dedicated room for euthanasia in veterinarian hospitals was once rare, but it's now becoming more common as vets recognize the importance of providing compassionate care:

> *We try and change the way in which this has been done, and I can remember that ten years ago, it was a novelty that a hospital had a room that's specifically set aside for euthanasia. It's nicer, it's not clinical…And now it's such an industry standard, a new hospital has two of them, and it doesn't feel like it's nearly enough.*

We also discussed the challenges faced by veterinary professionals, such as burnout and compassion fatigue. Brandon highlighted the significant burnout rate in the industry is often due to dealing with difficult cases, making euthanasia decisions, and managing clients' grief:

> *The average lifespan for someone working in the field as a veterinary technician is likely five years, and the program is three years, so they are in the vet world for less than ten years. You're only really dealing with sick pets most of the time. The doctors have that in some way, but their investment in a clinic is so significant that I think it feels way more dire for them if they realize that they're not handling it well.*

> *And I think people don't understand burnout either; it is a real thing, and you might not even be able to recognize it that that's happening to you. And then you have people come in who don't want to spend money on treatment…That's been a big part of where people get burned out. We're here to help and sometimes we have no means to help because people don't always put us in a good position to be able to help.*

To address these challenges, Brandon's hospital has integrated a social worker into their team to support both staff and clients in managing emotions and grief, reflecting a more holistic approach to veterinary care:

> *Our social worker is available for staff and for clients. Oftentimes, when we know clients are going to struggle, or when it looks like it's a particularly difficult case, we'll say, 'You have the opportunity to talk to her, and she will do follow-up work and sometimes six sessions or so with families.'*

> *The model used to be that the doctors just figured it out, and you worked with people through their grief. And it is a challenge when this is the fourth time you're dealing with it that day…If you have a team that can support that client, you can go back to treating patients. So that model has worked phenomenally well for us.*

The interview also covered the challenges of dealing with complicated health issues in pets, where clear answers or effective treatments may not always be available. It's important to have realistic expectations and provide caring support throughout our pets' journeys, understanding that some conditions may not have easy solutions.

Brandon mentioned how, especially in oncology, they often encounter cases where pets require palliative care, instead of focusing on extending their life as much as possible. Despite regular veterinary check-ups and preventive care, some conditions can remain hidden until they become critical, leading to unexpected and tough decisions about treatment options and financial concerns for pet owners.

He shared a common situation where pets may not show signs of illness until it's too late. He explained that animals naturally avoid showing vulnerability:

> *In prey species, where they never let on that they're sick at all…you can have a rabbit or a bird, they look perfectly fine, and they'll be dead two hours later. It's a deliberate defense mechanism so that they don't act weak. Dogs and cats do that to*

some extent. It's less to protect the owner and more just an instinctual behaviour to say, I'm fine, don't leave me behind from the pack, don't treat me differently…There are a lot of times where there's a very sudden, we want to say inexplicable decline, but there's usually a huge underlying factor that we discover. And then it's far too late to do anything about it because they didn't tell you.

Not all end-of-life situations result from a decision. Sometimes, the circumstances leave us powerless, such as a dog being hit by a car. When we feel robbed of that, it doesn't feel like it's the right time because we didn't have control over that situation. The lack of control feels particularly awful.

Brandon discussed how other resident pets may react when a fellow member passes away or is euthanized. He observed that dogs can often show signs of confusion and a search for the missing family member, suggesting their awareness of the absence. This can be particularly noticeable in homes with multiple pets, where the dynamics of the pack change after the loss. Each dog may express grief differently, ranging from visible distress to minimal reaction, based on their personality and the bond with the deceased:

It really would be wonderful if we could ever understand what they're thinking. Maybe one day we can. If people take their deceased pet home with them, they try and leave it with the other dogs for some time, and some of them are responsive, and some of them are not…Oftentimes when dogs realize that their family members are gone, they just lie there despondent, and they're always searching for them, and they don't really get what to do differently. They may come and sit with you and want to be held, and they may understand that you're upset and, therefore, they come to you and behave that way. It's so dependent on the animal. I've had dogs that just don't respond at all. I know people who, when one of their dogs passed away, their biggest concern was how to manage for the next couple of weeks. Like people, it's very individualized what that response is going to be.

It's important to recognize and validate our pets' emotions during times of loss while also understanding that, like humans, they will find their way through it. Brandon suggests pet owners can support their pets through grief by providing comfort and stability, paying attention to their cues, and offering reassurance.

It's widely acknowledged that pets have a significant impact on our lives. They give us motivation, reasons to get up in the morning and go for a walk, and to have something to care for. This makes a big difference in quality of life.

Brandon talked about how attitudes toward pets have changed over time. He mentioned that pets are now seen more as beloved family members rather than just animals. He expressed optimism for a shift in how society understands and supports grief related to pet loss, raising the importance of having open discussions about this type of grief. As pets are increasingly considered integral parts of families, he believes that openly grieving for them will become more normal and accepted in the future. He spoke about the importance of memorializing our pets after they have passed:

> *It's really important to a lot of people to honour that relationship and what their pet gave to them through their life. They want to do something dignified for them in death in the same way that you would for any other important member of the family…It is a reminder of what that dog was, what his life was like, and why this mattered…It's a very personal decision.*

He noted there are numerous commercial options for this ranging from urns to jewelry to customized Christmas ornaments. By commemorating our pets through various means, we can express our gratitude for the joy they brought into our lives while also preserving their legacies. For many of us, the opportunity to memorialize our pets serves as a form of closure. As well, it provides a space for us to openly express our feelings and emotions about the significance of the relationship, which may not always be accepted in other contexts.

Brandon emphasized the need for early and open communication about sensitive topics in veterinary care to reduce stress and grief for both pet owners and professionals. He feels that planning ahead for euthanasia can be a way to honour and celebrate our pet's lives, stressing that these decisions stem from love and mercy. He shared that big emotions can erupt when euthanasia is unexpected, such as with young animals or sudden illnesses, which can be particularly hard for pet owners to handle:

> *Plan ahead if you have the opportunity to take that time, do it. You know after the fact is always going to feel like it's too short. It's always going to feel like it was never enough, and really, there should be no guilt about it. We always feel like we could have done more. We always feel like we should have done something different.*

Brandon stressed the value of viewing euthanasia as a compassionate act that grants our pets a peaceful departure without prolonged suffering. He encouraged making space for the idea that euthanasia is a loving decision made in our pet's best interest:

> *Euthanasia really is an act of mercy. It's the last thing you get to do for your pet. If there's guilt attached to that grief, it really isn't worth it. I wish that it was easier for people to understand; we're not out there judging them for those things. We see it for the good that it is, to be able to offer, and that's the journey that the doctors and the vets are there to help you with. They're not in this because they're out there to euthanize pets. They're there because they know it's a gift that you get to give them. I think that people are way too hard on themselves about it.*

Both Dr. Titcombe's and Brandon's messages align with themes in this book regarding celebrating our pet's life and navigating our grieving process with compassion. Their core message is to relieve ourselves from the guilt and shame we sometimes carry regarding euthanasia, viewing it as a compassionate act rather than just a loss. They validate that the grieving process for our pets is the same as for humans, and this loss hurts regardless of whether or not there was an opportunity to have a say in their end-of-life circumstances.

When we recall our pets' lives with celebration, love, and companionship, we can cherish the experiences we shared with them, drawing attention to honouring their life and legacy. It's okay for us to feel grief, but we also need to let go of the pain that we no longer need. We must honour our feelings, seek support from others who understand pet loss, and find healthy ways to cope with our emotions. This will help us to navigate the love, loss, and legacy of our dog.

We all did our best to provide a loving and comfortable life for our dog. We must now practice self-compassion.

The Story of Rosco: A Bond Like No Other

Rosco was a beloved companion to his owner and a constant presence in her life. His owner recounts how he accompanied her on every adventure and, at times, he acted as if he thought he was human by sharing meals with her and choosing to sleep on the pillow beside her!

At the age of 11 Rosco suddenly started to show signs of declining health. He started to have hearing loss and difficulties with his back legs. His owner tried to accommodate his needs by adding stairs for the couch, but his condition deteriorated rapidly. One day he started throwing up, then he lost the ability to walk and stopped drinking. All he wanted was to lie in the snow and lick it.

The decision to say goodbye and let Rosco go was a heart-wrenching one, but his owner was driven to end his suffering. She stayed by his side until the end, offering comfort and singing their special song, "You are my sunshine."

Turn Within: Did you have a special song or activity with your dog?

Self-Care Moment: Moments of Mastery

It's natural for us to feel overwhelmed by grief during times of loss. Moments of mastery lie within the depths of our sorrow, and exploring our strength and resilience can harness them as sources of empowerment for our journey. For this activity, follow the instructions below.

Scan the QR code to complete this Self-Care Moment:

CHAPTER THREE: *THE LOSS*

Losing My World as I Knew It

When Aura's life ended after a long-anticipated death, I lost part of my identity as the primary caregiver of a dog with a heartbreaking, progressive illness.

I always knew I would likely live longer than her and expected that she would pass away one day. I did not expect this to happen when she was ten years old, nor was I prepared to cope with her intense needs. I watched her physical and cognitive capacities slip away over the years. I slowly lost the experience of her happy tail wags greeting me at the door, and her following me around the house from room to room. My house was full of love, and children, and other dogs, and at the same time, it felt empty with her gone.

I questioned if she was angry that I decided on euthanasia after years of her decline. At times, I accused myself of not loving her enough to keep her here longer. I called myself selfish, cruel, and a hypocrite. Obsessive thoughts followed me through my days: *She knew she was loved to the end. How could this happen to me? I did all the right things. Was I a bad dog mom? Was she even sick? Maybe I made it up that she was sick because I was so stressed out. Could I have somehow stopped her decline and fixed her? I was supposed to care for her, and I killed her!*

I was preoccupied with her suffering and, at the same time, had the conflicting message that her death was my fault. Technically, I called the vet, I invited them in, and I allowed them to administer the medications. But did I kill my dog? Deep down, I knew the answer was no, but I struggled to accept a reality where I did not, or could not, keep her here. So, the only acceptable answer I could come up with was that it was my fault.

The therapist side of me understands that the self-blaming part of me was actually trying to protect me, not torture me. It was trying to avoid the feeling of being out of control in my somewhat unpredictable world, which felt scary!

Although it was difficult, going through this phase was necessary for me to process my grief. I had to accept that she was gone for good; it was permanent, and I had to learn to live with this new reality. It didn't matter that I had lots of notice. I still had to come to the full realization of my loss. Eventually, I came to accept that my decision for euthanasia was not a betrayal—it was an act of love. I chose her need for peace, over my need to keep her here.

Turn Within: In an attempt to cope with your loss, what are some of the untrue stories that played in your mind?

What I Lost

I had dogs in childhood, and they were my siblings and playmates. Aura was my first dog as an adult, and she felt very different for me. Walking the neighbourhood became a whole new experience because, suddenly, I was a dog owner. I was approached with kindness by other humans just for walking down the street! People would stop us, say hello, and ask to pet her.

When Aura became part of our family, I was dealing with a lot: navigating a failed marriage, co-parenting challenges, questioning my parenting abilities, and struggling to connect with peers at university and with other parents. Most of my friend circle consisted of happily married women who didn't face the same issues I did, like frequent calls from the school principal or co-parenting conflicts like mine. They were as supportive as they could be, but they couldn't truly grasp my experience as a single mom dealing with these challenges. I often felt like my struggles provided them a window into an unusual world they couldn't relate to. I felt alone and judged by society in general. This left me feeling ashamed of my situation.

Aura helped to fill the void of these losses. Yes, my children gave me purpose and showed me love and affection. Yes, my boyfriend and now current husband was kind and listened to my every need. Yes, my friends and family were available to help—if I asked for it. These were all protective factors in my life, but Aura offered me something that my human support network could not. With her I felt accepted every day, every second she was around me. As simple as it sounds, at a time when I was feeling ostracized as a single mom, being a dog owner helped me feel like I finally belonged again—somewhere.

When Aura died, she was no longer physically here. That primary loss was obvious to everyone. What wasn't as obvious were the secondary losses of me yearning for her warm welcome at the door, looking forward to her announcement of spring, and noticing how empty the house was, even when full of children and other dogs. A secondary loss is what comes after the primary loss; it is no longer having a world as it was. While primary losses, such as the fact of death, are often recognized and considered more acceptable to grieve by others, secondary losses can be much more invisible and can flow from unexpected areas such as a sense of purpose or connections. The secondary losses torture us again and again by reminding us they are gone.

No one missed Aura like I was missing her. For a year and a half, I watched her decline, and I cared for her needs with love. I gladly owed her that. When she passed, I lost my job as her caretaker and protector. One might think that I was relieved to no longer be on call to make sure she was not going to walk into the pool or over the edge of the stairs. In some ways, I was relieved, but the void was unbearable. I had other dogs at home, so dog parks and dog-related social media groups still applied to my identity. I had other dogs to feed and walk, but those everyday activities suddenly felt less bright and were constant reminders that she wasn't here. I yearned for Aura to be here.

At least I could still go on dog walks; I can only imagine the immense void I would have felt without other dogs in my home. Every aspect of my life that involves dogs would have taken on a different significance: visits to parks, coming home, grocery shopping, relaxing in the backyard, social interactions, and even answering the doorbell. If I were no longer a dog owner, a large part of my identity would have shifted, and I would have felt disconnected from the dog-owning community in society. Even with maintaining the title of dog owner, the loss of Aura still caused profound pain.

Space, Time, & Attachment

In Andrew Huberman's podcast, The Huberman Lab, he offers insight into the world of neuroscience in a practical and accessible format. In his episode titled *The Science & Process of Healing From Grief,* he explains how understanding grief involves delving into three factors mapped in our consciousness related to attachment: space, time, and closeness. He states, "Those three dimensions of space, time, and closeness are what establish very close bonds with people, and are what require remapping and reorganization within our emotional framework and our logical framework, when we lose somebody." According to Huberman, space and time are regarding the where we know our loved one to exist, and when we will see them next. When we left for work every day, we likely missed our dog, but we did not grieve their absence all day. This is because we knew where they were and when we'd see them again. Closeness is about how connected or attached we are to them. It is how our relationship is wired regarding our sense of safety and security in the world. Let's dig a little deeper into these concepts.

Space

The dimension of space in this context relates to how we process grief physically and spiritually. Our bonds with people, pets, or things are like maps in our minds, and when someone or something we care about is no longer with us, we often feel a sense of longing.

Our mind tells us they are close yet out of reach. This is because the connection to that someone or something was originally encoded as forever important. As we cannot find them in the dimension of space, our mind takes a while to fully comprehend that they are gone. This is especially true when the loss involves death, as we do not have tangible and scientific proof of what actually happens to the essence of a life After-Death.

At first, we may keep expecting our dog to be sleeping in the corner of the room where their dog bed is or to greet us at the door when we come home, only to experience disappointment. The early period of bereavement is when we feel the most grief, because our brain is trying to make sense of where they are now.

Our brain has encoded them as everlasting in our mind, but they are physically gone, so both truths cause disorientation and confusion. Allowing ourselves to envision and accept where they are now, can help our brain accept that both truths can coexist.

Time

As our brain has encoded our dog's existence as forever in our space, our mind anticipates encountering them again. Our brain is trying to resolve the issue of them not being in our space, and also not knowing when we will see them again. The notion that we will never encounter them physically again is a very difficult concept to accept and process. Each time our mind expects their presence and we are let down, it is incredibly painful.

We need continued repetition to help us resolve the issue of time. Only then will our brain finally update to the more accurate prediction that our dog has departed this physical space—

forever. It makes sense that our brain favours the idea of our dog being here with us, so it will keep predicting what it has encoded as reliable and favourable for us. It needs time and repetition to remap, so we must search for self-compassion.

The fastest way to do this is to allow ourselves to feel our grief however it shows up, and connect to these feelings again and again. With each reminder, our brain slowly finds ways of relating to our new world reality without them here. Our neurons will eventually reorganize and remap so that our brain can predict differently. We cannot think our way out of our emotional pain, we must wait for it to happen naturally.

Closeness (Connection and Attachment)

This dimension concerns our emotional bond—our attachment to our dog. After a loss, we perceive our connection to be severed, and this is terrifying and painful! However, it is important to remember that our connection, our attachment, is never taken away; it is beautifully transformed. At first, this new form of connection is upsetting and painful, but eventually, our brain finds a way to remap and reorient to this new relationship in a way that offers personal growth and deeper connection.

Honouring our previous connection with our dog can help us rewire our new sense of attachment. This involves remembering the loving times we had and fully feeling our grief in the present moment. Some people allow themselves to only do this during certain times of the day with set times or rituals This can be especially helpful if we need to be fully present and alert at work, or to cook, drive, or parent. Others prefer to notice their loss as much as possible throughout their day, and this is fine as long as we can still function in the necessities of daily life and care for ourself.

What is important is that we make space and time to be present with our grief, and there are tools we can practice to help us with this. Some examples are deep breathing and meditation, which help us by calming our nervous system. When we practice techniques like this on a regular basis, our nervous system is able to move in and out of states more easily. As mentioned earlier, this is called vagal tone. We can also keep in mind that when our cortisol levels are regulated and we've been sleeping well, our body can work more effectively. Getting adequate sunshine early in the day can also help us.

Even though we logically know our dog has passed, the search for our dog is instinctual. This deep-rooted feeling of yearning stems from the closeness we formed with our dog.

Through this rich connection we created an internal representation of them, an expectation about their presence, and their physical proximity to us. At times, they made us feel that the world was predictable and safe. After they died, our mental map and internal representation of them were disrupted.

We might catch ourselves saying that we weren't that close, and that their absence doesn't bother us. This likely happens because it's just so overwhelming to accept they are no longer here physically. It's important to remember that this is not helpful, as the attachment is there—we cannot deny this!

So, which dimension should we prioritize to remap: space, time, or closeness? Well, we can't control our attachment, and it has not been severed. Our ongoing need for connection is real. Our love is real. The pain, is real. We have more control over helping our brain to remap connections regarding time and space—our brain is already doing its best to naturally rewire our connection. The goal is to tolerate holding our love for our dog while at the same time accepting they are gone in space and time. This process will automatically be ongoing and oscillating forever, but I promise you it will not always feel disturbing to think of your dog.

It's important to focus on honouring the intensity of our attachment, which we talk more specifically about in Chapter 5 when we explore continuing the bond. When we honour our love for them, we respect and strengthen our connection to our dog without downplaying its importance. This allows for our attachment and connection to adjust in time and space.

The grieving process is all about accommodating our new

world realities and reshaping our mental maps. As explored earlier neurochemicals, hormones, and our unique attachment styles can all influence our grieving process. There is no right or wrong way, and most of us find a way on our own without professional support. That said, avoiding people, places, and emotions makes it harder for our brain to make new pathways. Being gentle with ourselves and allowing our emotions to flow without judgment are crucial in navigating our grief.

We all deserve self-compassion and inner peace, regardless of the circumstances. The *Self-Care Moments* throughout this book aim to help you with this.

Rules of Grief

Robin Shapiro is a psychotherapist, trainer, and author of many books related to working with trauma, attachment issues, dissociation, anxiety, and depression. Her books and clinical guidance have been instrumental in my growth as a therapist. She writes the following as a guide for grief and mourning:

1. *It always hurts more than you think it should.*
2. *It always lasts longer than you (and others) think it ought.*
3. *It makes you tired, cranky, stupid or feeling hopeless.*
4. *Avoid it and it stays terrible, creates depression and/or useless busyness.*
5. *Feel it all and it gets better.*

Knowing what to expect can ease some of our discomfort. It's also helpful to understand that we will go through the range of feelings many times, especially whenever there is a life milestone or celebration. We may notice feeling sad, angry, depressed, or calm, then back through various states to exhaustion. Feelings may come and go many times, especially during significant life events or celebrations. We should expect these waves of feelings, as this will help us brace through them. Know that the waves will pass.

We might feel relieved and sad at the same time. These conflicting feelings may create a sense of shame so remember, it's okay to have mixed emotions because relationships are complex!

Sometimes we create stories to cope with our loss, such as blaming ourselves for not preventing it. This is how our system tries to regain control in a situation that feels helpless.

Grief can also bring up past losses, making our current loss feel even more overwhelming. Addressing any related trauma is crucial for healing. Accepting and adapting to our new reality is not just one moment of time—it is a process that involves many moments of growth.

It is comforting to have someone acknowledge and understand our emotional pain with empathy. No one else can take on our grief or try to fix it for us, and sometimes we need extra help.

Finding meaning in life after our loss is also a significant part of the healing journey. This is about using our grief as a source of personal growth. Basic activities such as walking, running, and cross-country skiing are activities which can help let the feelings flow. We cover many more suggestions throughout this book.

Loss of the Assumptive World

We all have basic assumptions or core beliefs that help us to feel grounded, secure, stabilized, and oriented in the world. Loss of the assumptive world refers to our world not being as we believe it to be, a wake-up call when we experience loss. We humans like to have predictability and consistency in our lives. We design our world as one that we can control and predict the future based on previous experiences. Our minds naturally create assumptions, expectations, and beliefs based on the rules we've learned and internalized. Feeling secure in our space, time, and connections is an ideal path to navigating life and protecting ourselves. However, experiences like death and trauma can disrupt our beliefs, challenging our sense of how the world works.

Ronnie Janoff-Bulman, a social psychologist and retired professor at the University of Massachusetts, is well known for her book *Shattered Assumptions: Toward a New Psychology of Trauma*. She researched how people with trauma cope, and the underlying shift in how they see the world due to their traumatic experiences. What she proposed were three primary categories of how we tend to assume that our world exists:

1. Benevolence of the World

We may believe the world and people are kind, categorizing them as good or bad. When our worldview is that people and the world are generally good, we also tend to think that misfortune is relatively uncommon and that the world is helpful, and caring. We expect that bad things won't happen to us because the world and people are generally good.

2. Meaningfulness of the World

This is where we go about life believing we have control. If the world and life are meaningful, predictable, and fair, then what happens to us depends on what we do. We might tell ourselves that how things turn out is decided by justice, and that people get what they deserve. So if we are a good and decent person, bad things won't happen to us.

Perhaps we believe that what happens in the world is distributed by control. If that's the case, then we feel we can minimize our vulnerability by engaging in proper behaviours. We might tell ourselves that we live in a world with consistent and predictable social laws involving justice and controllability. But sometimes terrible things can still happen no matter what we do or what rules we make up. This is hard for us to process and understand

We also might try to convince ourselves that what happens to and around us is distributed by chance. We may convince ourselves that there is no way of making sense of why certain things happen to certain people, and nothing can be done to protect us from negative outcomes. This outlook can invite a sense of helplessness.

3. Worthiness of Self

We may believe that we and our loved ones are worthy, where surely, our moral character will serve as protection in a just world. In this case, we justify outcomes by believing that those of us with low self-worth are more vulnerable to a negative outcome, and goodness determines positive outcomes. This time, our focus is on necessary behaviours to control our outcomes instead of whether or not we can control them. Here, we believe that those with the most exemplary behaviour will be the least vulnerable to bad things. Therefore, we tend to expect that although sometimes things are out of our control, bad things do not happen to good people.

We may perceive ourselves as generally lucky and therefore protected from ill fortune. From this perspective, the world operates by chance, and a lucky person is somehow protected from bad things.

These three assumptions are a large part of our worldview and are most likely to be altered after we experience a traumatic event. Unfortunately, we tend to think we can control and predict more than we actually can. When loss happens, we can lose our understanding of our world as we know it, which can be catastrophic to our internal mental schema. Like a glitch in the movie *The Matrix*, our internal system does not know how to cope. The program carries on the best it can, but the code is trying to work itself out in the background.

When we lose our assumptive world, we tend to self-blame or shame. Although the following thoughts might be activating to read, we must acknowledge they come from an emotional part of our brain and not from logic. The *Self-Care Moment: Letting Go of What-Ifs* near the end of this chapter can be a helpful guide to more positive and accurate thinking. These irrational thoughts can include:

- *I shouldn't be alive; it should have been me.*
- *I killed my dog because I agreed to euthanasia.*
- *Owners are supposed to protect their animals; it's my fault.*
- *This happened to me, so I am bad.*

Guilt and shame can make it hard to accept our loss and understand our emotions. If we believe our moral values were compromised, we might feel an overwhelming sense of responsibility. Survivor's guilt is where we feel guilty for being alive while others are not.

We may get preoccupied with why it happened, whose fault it was, and who should be responsible moving forward. We may question our faith or need help navigating new goals or purposes.

It can be traumatizing when we find ourselves preoccupied with the suffering of our loved one. This is especially true if the deceased did suffer. We might get stuck focusing on what we felt in the moment of the loss instead of being able to process what actually happened. We may ruminate on unhelpful or untrue thoughts such as:

- *She was in so much pain, and I wasn't there to stop it.*
- *He was trapped, and I didn't save them.*

- *She was so scared, and I didn't fix it.*

If this is you, I imagine your journey so far has been very difficult. I know this is hard, but try to remind yourself that they are at peace now. You are reading this book because you loved and cared for them deeply. Your dog knew you loved them, and they brought with them their own memories of your love.

Let's take a quick break now to practice breathing and strengthen vagal tone.

Breathe in through your nose and belly, then all the way out through your mouth. Again though your nose, all the way out slowly through your mouth. Last time in—and out with a sigh through your mouth. Wiggle your feet and notice your seat supporting your body.

We will eventually adapt to how we love our dog in their absence, because our attachment is never lost. At first, it is painful for us to love someone who is no longer here because this is a new concept for us to follow through with. We can adapt by exploring who we are now that they are gone, and identify the new realities that we are forced to accept. This does not mean giving up our attachment. We will always love them; we will always want them here—but the pain will not always feel so intense.

Know that pain is not required to keep loving our dog. Feeling then giving up this pain is not letting go of our love. If anything, this is the path to reconnection. Keeping our pain and resisting acceptance of the new world does not give us more control—that path ultimately robs us of the transformative gifts that grief can provide.

Self-Care Moment: Confronting Negative Beliefs

Our mind struggles to accept reality when we feel powerless, helpless, or a loss of control. Sometimes, our mind tries to cope by placing blame or shame on ourselves. Have a look at the list of negative beliefs below and see if you recognize any of them circulating in your mind. Then, have a look at the positive cognitions to redirect yourself towards self-compassion. Add more as you see fit and come back to this list as you need to.

Scan the QR code to complete this Self-Care Moment:

The Story of Dublin: Unconditional Love

Dublin wasn't just a pet; he was a furry confidant who shared in his owner's life journey for over a decade. Their bond began when Dublin came home from a pet store, then continued through the ups and downs of high school, the challenges of university life, moments of heartache, and the losses of beloved grandparents.

At 12 years old, Dublin's final days were a painful blur of seizures, a dwindling appetite, and an inability to move his swollen body. His last night was spent on a large dog bed with the whole family sleeping on the floor beside him, giving cuddles.

In addition to the heartbreaking loss of Dublin in 2021, his passing coincided with the onset of yet another pandemic lockdown. This left a sense of isolation that words could not fill. At first Dublin's owner felt a mix of sadness and uncertainty, wondering if they had done everything right for him in his last weeks.

As she reflected on Dublin's legacy, his owner found peace in their memories of unconditional love and acceptance. Each wag of his tail, cuddle, and shared moment became a treasured memory; a testament to the profound impact Dublin had on her life. This experience also sparked a desire to give back to the community by rescuing another dog later on, and supporting others going through grief.

Dublin's owner wants readers to understand that while he

may be physically gone, his spirit and memories will always remain. She finds comfort in her belief that our pets and memories will always be with us, a reassuring reminder that they never truly leave us.

Turn Within: Are you giving yourself permission to feel?

A Ripple Effect

It was almost a year since Aura had died, yet I was still having moments of disappointment when she was not part of the barking symphony greeting me at the door. All around me were messages suggesting that, by then, I should have moved on, and that her life was not as valuable as a human's. I suspect people assumed that because I had other dogs in the home, I was fine. Rarely did anyone ask, and I was not comfortable expressing my sadness anyway.

Disenfranchised grief is when grief is stigmatized or seen as unacceptable to express. This type of grief is common with loss by suicide, miscarriage, or non-pregnancy. It can also apply to the loss of a pet, as society does not always acknowledge the depth of this type of loss, and we can often feel like it is not acceptable to grieve this loss as big as it feels.

Losing a dog might mean losing the equivalent of a partner, best friend, and child. For some people, the unconditional love of a dog is their only source of acceptance, a sense of purpose, and reassurance that life is going to be okay. We may no longer have a walking buddy or hold the title of dog owner. Without a dog, the world can feel dark and pointless.

Grief touches every corner of our lives. The primary loss is the death itself—the sudden absence of the dog we cherished, the empty space they left behind, and the shattered possibility of making future memories. This often hits us hard, like a gust of wind knocking us off our feet. This type of loss is easier for others to see, and they are more likely to offer condolences.

But grief doesn't stop there; it sends ripples throughout our life and lifespan, causing secondary losses that are often overlooked but just as profound. These losses are like storm clouds rolling in, and include changes to our routines, roles, and identity. As these are more difficult for others to recognize and offer support, these areas are more likely where we need additional emotional assistance, like therapy.

With grief, a portal opens to all past loss, awakening all unresolved trauma and sadness we've faced in the past. When the death of a loved one brings up memories of past hurts, we become even more emotionally fragile.

In essence, grief is a journey of all loss—both seen and unseen, new and old. By understanding our loss, we can give ourselves permission to grieve not only the death but also the full consequences of the death in our lives. When we identify secondary losses, we can better prepare for the challenges that lie ahead, including adjusting to a new reality and accepting support. Recognizing the changes in our lives will lead to navigating our grief with more resilience and self-compassion.

At times, a loss can be so overwhelming that it makes it hard for us to remember the good times we shared with our dog. It's like those happy memories are hidden away because the pain of the loss is too intense to bear. The clouds are hiding the sunshine leaving us feeling stuck and in the dark.

Self-Care Moment:
Reflection on Loss & Change

Reflecting on our loss and the changes it has brought into our lives helps us realize the full consequences of it. Then, we can start rebuilding our connection within our new world reality.

Take as much time as you need to complete this activity. Remember to be gentle with yourself, and feel whatever emotions come up during this process. Use deep breathing or other grounding exercises as needed.

Scan the QR code to complete this Self-Care Moment:

The Story of Bailey: Storm on the Horizon

Bailey is the most pugly dog I've ever met. I describe "pugly" as a term for pugs with features that might typically be seen as undesirable yet are also undeniably adorable. Years ago, she was found in a garbage dumpster along with her brother; both were in dire medical need after they were rescued. Unfortunately, her brother did not survive his medical interventions.

Bailey embodies a larger bone structure, and big bulgy eyes that you can't quite tell which way she is looking. Due to serious dental surgery, her bottom teeth, some of the few left, often protrude up and over her snout, where they perfectly frame her pink hanging tongue.

My fur sister is very particular with her humans, and I try not to let it bother me that my father likely favours her company over mine. She loves her food and naps, and is such a gentle soul. After my parents adopted her, she immediately became a second dent in my dad's favourite chair.

My mother continued working for many years after he retired, so Bailey has offered him constant companionship and routine. Bailey has been a reason for him to get up in the morning, walk around the block, and be social with neighbours. She has provided him with unconditional love and a constant message of

"I choose you" and "You are so special to me." She is his porch buddy, and when he leaves the home, she is known to sit patiently by the door waiting for him.

Sometimes I pup-sit her when my parents go on vacation. When she visits, my resident pack has always respected her for who she is, and they are always happy to greet her. After hours of waiting at my front door for my dad to return, Bailey will often concede that my affection will temporarily support her needs. This involves her demanding she be lifted on the couch so that she can meld her body as close to me as possible, just like with my dad. If I stop petting her, she taps her paw on my lap to make it very clear that this is my new assigned role. Bailey is a very special dog.

We don't know for sure how old Bailey is, but we know she was an adult when she entered our lives. She's always had issues with her hips and legs, but for years, she has enjoyed walks with my dad. Stairs have always been painful for her, so my dad has lovingly carried all twenty-eight pounds of her up and down these obstacles. Where we live in Canada it is often too cold for him to walk around the block, but never too icy for his Bailey-Boo to get fresh air down narrow steps to the backyard!

About a year ago, I noticed Bailey starting to look off into space, frozen for a few seconds. It almost looked like her head would twitch. As a typical pug, she was always hungry, but it seemed she started to forget that she had eaten and would bark at her empty bowl even minutes after a meal.

More recently, while I was pup-sitting her, I witnessed her barely able to walk across the room. Standing was a wobbly uncertainty. Sometimes, she'd wander aimlessly, and it was hard to tell if she was not responding when we called her name because of selective hearing, or if this was an indication that she no longer knew her name. In retrospect, I'm fairly sure she was experiencing regular mini-seizures, and she has definitely lost weight, which is odd for her.

Her barking has now become constant, like a smoke detector that needs its battery replaced. I remember what it was like to not fully realize the circumstances of my dog's health even though I was right there. This can be especially true when our dog's medical issues are slowly progressing.

When my parents returned from their last vacation, I voiced what I had observed during Bailey's visit with us. I could tell this was a difficult topic for them to absorb. My Dad was visibly upset with the idea, and my heart broke for him. I know that Bailey is so much more than just a dog in their lives.

When the moment arrives for Bailey to cross over the rainbow, my heart will ache as she holds a special place in my life, like a sister. I'm already feeling the weight of grief, especially for my dad. While I believe in his strength and resilience, imagining him facing the profound emptiness and tumultuous waves of grief sends chills down my spine. I wish I could ease his pain, but nobody is immune to grief. Witnessing my dad's connection with Bailey and the emotions he carries just beneath the surface, has deepened my connection to his humanity.

Turn Within: Notice how it felt when your dog showed you, "I choose you" and "You are so special to me." Now, notice how they must have felt when you returned their love every day.

Anticipated Grief

Anticipated grief is when we start to feel grief before the loss actually happens. Examples of this can be when our dog is very sick or getting older, if we have a loved one living with addiction, or if we are diagnosed with a terminal illness.

We can prepare ourselves for the inevitable sadness that comes with grief. One way to do this before or after a loss is by working on our vagal tone, where we practice being present and aware of our body. As discussed, we can do this by practicing deep breathing exercises that focus on slowing down our heart rate. This is because when we breathe out slowly our heart rate slows down too, and this helps our nervous system practice. It like practicing a fire drill, for when the waves of grief eventually come.

Another tool is practicing containment. Containing our grief from time to time is healthy so we can function. Trying to ignore or distract ourselves from grief by numbing with substances like alcohol or drugs only makes it harder for us in the long run. Those who avoid accommodating to their new world, or try to distract themselves with work or other behaviours won't move through grief as well or as adaptively as those who face it directly.

Pretending it's not going to happen is counterproductive, and full disclosure, strengthening your vagal tone won't help you avoid feeling grief. We can't stop the grief from happening, but we can increase our resilience to handle it better.

Knowing that grief is coming and taking steps to prepare your body does not mean it will feel easy. We can't stop the grief from happening, but we can increase our resilience to handle it better. We all must go through the storm to heal and grow, and grieving is an important part of life. By facing grief head-on and building up our ability to cope with it, we can move through it in a healthier and more adaptive way.

Containment

When we are facilitating a meeting, driving, taking care of children, or cooking a meal, our sense of overwhelm with sadness is usually not helpful. Although there is no such thing as a good or a bad feeling, sometimes we need to contain our upset so that we can carry on throughout certain aspects of our day. Think of feelings in terms of helpful vs unhelpful in a moment, instead of good or bad.

Imagine that every time you felt an upsetting emotion it was the equivalent of an unwanted package being delivered to your door. You know that in the package is a movie of something you don't ever want to think about again, so you put it in the basement and forget it is there. Multiple times a day this happens, and this is effective for a while. One day, you are reading a book in your living room, and you start to hear sounds coming from the basement level. Somehow, one of the movies are staring to play on a projector. You open the door and yell at it to be quiet, and it does—for a while. The sounds become louder and louder until you can no longer function. You go to deal with the mess down there, but it is so full you can barely make your way through the space.

These overwhelming feelings are not bad. They all have a purpose and deserve to be seen and heard. Due to how they were stored and then ignored, they were never dealt with and just piled up.

There is a more sustainable way to deal with waves of difficult emotions. Dosing our exposure to our grief is part of adapting to our loss, and can prevent us from feeling flooded. The following *Self-Care* Moment invites you to use an imaginal container. I offer this powerful tool to all my clients and use it myself. It is great as a self-regulation tool for every day, and helpful at the end of a therapy session in case we don't have time to resolve a difficult topic. Compared to stuffing boxes in the basement, this is a much healthier practice to assist with daily functioning.

Self-Care Moment: Container

This *Self-Care Moment* is a meditation adapted from EMDR basic training. It is being offered to you as a resource for containing big waves of emotion so that you can function day to day during your grief recovery.

Listen to the guided meditation here:

My Spaceships

As I listened to one of my clients give me an update on what was new and different since our last session, I noticed my breathing started to get faster. Attempting to remain composed and present, I shifted in my chair and visualized using my container. My client was crying because their dog had died unexpectedly. As I used my container, I was able to be with them fully to hold their grief instead of be flooded by my own. The session ended, and Aura's face popped into my mind. I had to use every tool in my toolbox to ground and contain before my next client. Feeling my sadness about Aura's death is healthy to feel, but not helpful when I'm trying to work.

When I got home my husband asked me how my day was. His question was the equivalent of unexpectedly opening a release valve! My unprocessed grief was manifesting as a sense of overwhelm, and I had the desire to numb. Since this time, I have sought additional support and worked through my trauma and grief. Even therapists need a therapist.

I'm open to sharing with you that my container is a spaceship that orbits the Earth. It never comes close to me. What's in it cannot escape, and it has to stay there and enjoy the view of the stars and the Earth from a far distance until I choose to check in. The deal is that the unhelpful stuff stays in the container, and I practice self-care. In return, I deal with what's in the container when it is a more helpful time and I'm feeling resilient. This is an excellent tool for my personal mental health, and I see it help others all the time. I even have a second smaller spaceship docked to store my professional stuff.

My spaceships are in great working order because first of all, I built them that way, and second, I practice self-care on a regular basis which helps to maintain them. I highly recommend using a container of your own.

Depression & Trauma

Grief can sometimes look and feel like depression, but there are key differences. The psychological and physiological process of grief in the brain and body is unique compared to depression.

As explored earlier, grief involves seeking, yearning, and longing for what was lost. There is also a deep desire for relief from the emotional pain of grief. With depression, there is little energy or motivation to move out of the existing state.

During bereavement, we oscillate between a range of emotions and experience a yearning for our loved one. With depression, there is very little positive emotions, and more of a general sadness than yearning for a specific thing.

Common symptoms of grief and depression can include sleep and appetite disturbance, and intense sadness. With depression, the feelings of sadness and despair are accompanied by a lost sense of self-esteem.

Some of us may experience major depression following a loss. This is where pre-existing feelings of worthlessness are intensified. We may notice thoughts of self-harm or suicide, and our mental or physical activities may slow down. We may lose interest in doing things we once found pleasurable, and have difficulty functioning day-to-day.

Medications can help with the energy levels of depression, but if the sadness is due to grief these medicines might not be as effective. As well, being offered medication for the state of grief can once again send the message that our feelings are not manageable. Many find that approaching grief naturally is most efficient.

When we experience loss, whether it's the death of a loved one or another significant life change, past traumas and unresolved emotional wounds can resurface. This can feel overwhelming and challenging to navigate, but it's also an opportunity for growth and healing. In a supportive environment, the grieving process offers us the chance to confront and process past traumas.

At times, our grief can become incredibly overwhelming and even traumatic. It can bring feelings of disconnection from what or who we lost. The event of a loss can also be traumatic, where there is a significant disruption in our feelings of safety and predictability.

Trauma does not necessarily mean you have a diagnosis of Post Traumatic Stress Disorder (PTSD). It is a common initiation in life, and more likely to happen when we perceive a threat that we cannot avoid. This leads to feelings of helplessness and loss of control. These events overwhelm our system, and our memories are dysfunctionally stored. Remember the Velociraptor in the forest? Trauma always involves a loss, whether it's a loss of control, a person, a thing, or an identity. Therefore, trauma always activates loss.

So, in every traumatic experience there's an element of grief, but not all grief is traumatic. Unresolved loss can consume us. This has a cumulative effect on us, resulting our mind and body being out of harmony.

Effects on the Body

Dr. Gabor Maté is a respected physician who is an expert in areas such as addiction, stress, childhood development, and mental health. He has written many insightful books, and his informative message has likely helped millions of people. In his book, *The Body Says No: The Cost of Hidden Stress*, he discusses the connection between our psychological state and the body. He provides insight into the mind-body link between illness and health when he writes:

> *Attachment is our connection with the world. In the earliest attachment relationships, we gain or lose the ability to stay open, self-nurturing and healthy. In those early attachment bonds, we*

learned to experience anger or to fear it and repress it. There we developed our sense of autonomy or suffered its atrophy. Connection is also vital to healing. Study after study concludes that people without social contact — the lonely ones — are at greatest risk for illness. People who enjoy genuine emotional support face a better prognosis, no matter what the disease.

According to Dr. Maté, if we have learned to repress our feelings, our physical health may suffer. If we isolate ourselves during bereavement or hold back our emotions, we risk getting stuck in grief. It is important to grasp when to go it alone and when to accept support:

The core belief in having to be strong enough, characteristic of many people who develop chronic illness, is a defence. The child who perceives that her parents cannot support her emotionally had better develop an attitude of 'I can handle everything myself.' Otherwise, she may feel rejected. One way not to feel rejected is never to ask for help, never to admit 'weakness' — to believe that I am strong enough to withstand all my vicissitudes alone.

Although very influential and real, I see anger as a secondary emotion. At the core of anger is often sadness or fear.

Holding back or repressing anger can have significant effects on our health, especially on our immune system. When we bottle up our anger instead of expressing it in a healthy way, it can lead to autoimmune dysfunction. This means that our body's natural defence mechanisms, which protect us from illnesses and diseases, can become compromised.

Expressing anger helps us establish boundaries and recognize situations that may be harmful to us. By allowing ourselves to acknowledge and appropriately express our anger, we can safeguard our emotional and physical well-being. Just as the immune system protects us by recognizing harmful situations, healthy anger is meant to protect us through boundaries.

Sometimes it is helpful to temporarily contain our anger or to titrate how and when we express it. When contained or expressed in a healthy way, this serves as a protective factor. Repressing anger increases autoimmune dysfunction.

Furthermore, Dr. Maté describes factors that help us understand why grief feels so uncomfortable:

> *The research literature has identified three factors that universally lead to stress: uncertainty, the lack of information and the loss of control.*

This sounds a lot like grief! Grief brings uncertainty, and a lack of information regarding the well-being of our loved one. Now that their body has died or there is anticipation of this in the near future, we struggle with a lack of control over the situation.

Another interesting connection Dr. Maté mentions is how in-tune animals are with us, and that our connection is through the emotional parts of our brains:

> *People and their pets connect via shared brain structures that predate the development of the human frontal cortex with its apparatus of language and rationality. Animals and humans interact from their respective limbic systems, the brain's emotional parts. Unlike people, animals are acutely sensitive to messages from the limbic brain—both their own and that of their owners.*

The connection between humans and dogs is synchronized through emotion. Dogs are literally connected to us by feeling our feelings! They are so in tune with us that they know when we need emotional support. It is no wonder that when they are gone, we feel such a void!

Turn Within: How did your dog show they were in tune with you? Journal how that made you feel.

Allowing ourselves to fully experience and express our grief helps us heal from loss. This also assists us with recovering from underlying trauma that may have been affecting us for years.

Grief is hard on our body, so we must give it a break and treat it well. We're on a journey that invites us to acknowledge our pain, confront our past experiences, and ultimately find peace. By recognizing the connection between grief, trauma, and our body, we can approach our healing journey with compassion, understanding, and hope for the future.

Common Reactions to Loss

It is helpful to recognize grief for what it is. As I go through these common reactions, notice if you've seen any of them in yourself.

Feelings

When we experience grief, we can circulate through a variety of feelings such as overwhelmed, numb, or responsible for the circumstances surrounding the death. It is also common for death to make us worry about our own mortality and our ability to cope, or bring up fears about caring for ourselves in the future. A conflicting sense of relief and freedom may arise from caregiving responsibilities or witnessing suffering.

The weight of sadness and deep sorrow resulting from the absence of our loved one can hijack our existence. Fatigue and exhaustion from the emotional toll of grief can creep in, and feelings of helplessness and powerlessness can be all-consuming. Loneliness, social isolation, and a sense of broken attachment might accompany our yearning for their presence. We feel shock, disbelief, disorientation, and we might feel a sense of emotional detachment due to overwhelming feelings.

Sometimes anger emerges due to our lack of control of the outcomes and from feeling left behind. We might displace our anger toward the situation, or at others. When we continue feeling angry at ourselves we are leaning toward depression, and it may be time to consider seeking professional support.

Physical Symptoms

Grief can manifest physically in many ways. It might feel like tightness in our chest or throat, a hollowness or emptiness in our stomach, or an oversensitivity to noise. Our body may have lots of energy, a lack energy, or feel weak. We might experience shortness of breath, dry mouth, or physical pain. Sleep and appetite can be disturbed. We may find ourself crying uncontrollably, or not at all and keeping ourself overly busy.

Cognitive Reactions

It is common to experience confusion as a first reaction when we lose someone we love. It can be hard to accept they are gone, and nothing seems real. We might want to withdraw socially or avoid any reminder of our dog. We may become preoccupied or have obsessive thoughts about our dog, or the events leading up to the actual death. Some people even sense as if the deceased is present or watching, or they have vivid dreams of them.

Recognizing these varied responses can validate our experiences and guide us in seeking support. Keeping the deceased's belongings close may feel good, and revisiting locations significant to the relationship can help us to reminisce and feel connected. When we're more self-aware about what we're feeling, we can notice the need to use coping strategies.

Turn Within: What symptoms have you been experiencing?

The Story of Sheryl: Resilience and Love Beyond Loss

Sheryl was a first childhood pet who held a special place in her owner's heart. They shared many moments together where Sheryl would get dressed up in a hat and wear purses.

When circumstances led to a family move, Sheryl had to be sent to live with another family. This caused profound heartbreak for her owner, despite her parent's reassurance that Sheryl was thriving in her new home. Memories of dressing up Sheryl and enjoying playful moments together lingered for the rest of her childhood.

As an adult, Sheryl's owner found peace and happiness in welcoming Poochie, a new canine companion. At first, she was hesitant and unsure if she could form a similar deep connection, but Poochie quickly became a beloved friend and a source of comfort.

Dressing up Poochie in sweaters and hats brought smiles, reigniting loving memories of Sheryl. Through Poochie, her grief has come full circle as love knows no bounds.

Turn Within: How was your life changed for the better because of your dog?

Complicated Grief

When we get stuck with moving through grief, adapting and reorienting to our new reality is disrupted. This is sometimes called complicated grief, complicated mourning, unresolved traumatic grief, Persistent Complex Bereavement Disorder (PCBD), or Prolonged Grief Disorder (PGD). When this happens, we feel an intense longing for the deceased, and constantly think about our loved one with sadness and regret. Thoughts can be intrusive, empty and hopeless about the future, making it hard for us to move forward and feel balanced.

When we experience this stress long-term, we feel less resilient and struggle to contain our grief during day-to-day tasks. We might be experiencing complicated grief if we are unable to acknowledge or understand our loss, feel numb to our pain, or notice ourselves resisting to let go of the old world and accommodate for the new.

The Diagnostic and Statistical Manual of Mental Disorders (DSM) is a reference for diagnosing mental health conditions. It distinguishes a variety of conditions to better help us understand the differences between diagnoses regarding trauma and grief.

With Post-Traumatic Stress Disorder (PTSD), people avoid reminders of trauma. Main emotions of avoidance include fear, anxiety, anger, guilt, and shame.

In Persistent Complex Bereavement Disorder (PCBD), there's a strong focus on the loss and longing for the deceased. Characterized by intense and persistent grief reactions lasting beyond what is considered typical, this is often considered a form of complicated grief, similar to Prolonged Grief Disorder (PGD). Persistent Complex Bereavement Disorder typically involves a drive towards what was lost with an emotional response of yearning or emptiness.

It is possible to experience Post-Traumatic Stress Disorder regarding the traumatic aspects of the loss and Persistent Complex Bereavement Disorder at the same time. Both of these diagnoses have hope through therapeutic approaches such as self-care, psychotherapy, and pharmaceutical interventions. Moving forward with grief happens as we eventually internalize that our loved one is gone, identify and feel our feelings, and then develop a new relationship with ourself and the outside world. Only then will we have the full capacity to reinvest in life without our dog here.

There are a few situations that can influence the heaviness of our grief. Dogs are trained every day to save our lives from physical danger and medical issues, and they are also great at saving us from the dark stories that we play in our head. If our dog provided us with daily living support and we were dependent on them to help us through our day, then our quality of life has likely shifted without them here. If that happy wagging tail was the only thing that reminded us that we are lovable and have something to live for, then we were likely rescued by them, and had a deep reliance on their love. The more we depended on our dog emotionally or physically the heavier the grief, but this does not mean we are going to be stuck forever.

There are things we can do to help us become unstuck. The reality is we will grieve forever, but the intensity of our feelings will usually reduce over time with exposure and accommodation to the new world. To move through grief, we must acknowledge, accept, and assimilate the violation of our assumptive world. This process may or may not happen quickly. We can recover from trauma. With grief, however, we do not fully recover. Instead, we forever assimilate, adapt, and accommodate for the loss.

If you are stuck in complicated grief, feel you have experienced trauma, or are slipping into depression, especially if you have persistent feelings of guilt or worthlessness, it's important to seek support from professionals. It's okay to need more intervention and support!

Disenfranchised Grief

"I'm writing a book on grief and loss of a dog," I said, expecting a negative reaction. I was shocked when, time after time, the response was connection. Almost everyone I mentioned expressed that they or someone they know needs a book on this topic. I find it so interesting that we all accept that dogs have been enriching our lives for thousands of years, and we all know the loss of a loved one is painful, yet we haven't outwardly normalized the intensity of emotions with dog loss.

The truth is, grief and mourning someone else is experiencing makes most people uncomfortable. When we look at this from the perspective that grief invites all past loss, it makes sense that someone else's grief makes us want to run away! Many of us have felt this discomfort around others in bereavement; it's not a personal rejection.

To add to this, society seems to diminish the pain of pet loss, and this is called disenfranchised grief. Having our grief unrecognized can make us feel isolated and ashamed of our feelings. Dismissing the pain experienced when a dog dies has always boggled my mind. If we openly accept that pets bloom happiness inside of us, it doesn't make sense that we dismiss the grief that follows their loss! Once again, think of all the cat and dog videos that circulated during COVID-19 to "get us through hard times." No one ever questioned our dog's ability to make us feel loved when they were alive. It was acceptable for us to express love to them when they were here. It's disappointing that society questions the pain that comes with loss when this physical connection is gone.

During our moments of loss, others can sometimes say the most upsetting things. This might be because they cannot connect with our grief or because they are navigating the awkwardness of their own grief brought up by our situation. They may suggest we move on or get another dog. This is ridiculous because our connection and attachment to our dog cannot be removed or replaced!

This would never be suggested as a solution regarding the loss of a human loved one. Most of us would agree the following statements are rude and ridiculous, "So, have you thought about getting another friend yet? I'm sure there is another one out there," or, "You need to move on. She was a good sister, but she was just a sibling," or, "What do you mean you kept your partner's photo on the mantle? They're gone so you don't need it anymore; throw it out!"

When our human loved ones see the loss of our dog as "just a dog," our grief goes unwitnessed, and the pain deepens. We might start to feel isolated and want to hide our grief. This blocks us from getting the support we need, the very ingredient we need from our social circle to help us to grow.

We need emotional truths, not intellectual connections. All relationships are unique, so no one knows how we feel right now. When we receive messages from others that they are uncomfortable with our feelings, it suggests that we must pretend to feel differently than what we're feeling in the depths of our grief. When it is suggested that we should no longer be suffering simply because our loved one is no longer suffering, it dismisses our experience and our special bond. Yes it can be helpful to explore a sense peace within their peace, but emotions of grief are complex.

Unhelpful comments are often true attempts to soothe us, but they address the intellectual connections of our loss, and not our emotional truths. We are told to not feel bad, and to find a more acceptable feeling instead. What we need is for others to validate our feelings. We need to be heard, not fixed. Then, we can make our own intellectual decisions.

Whether people react in an unsupportive way because they do not understand the loss or because they are trying to avoid their own feelings of loss, this behaviour is not helpful. And I get it; even as a professional, I still say the wrong thing from time to time. We must try harder to support each other with all forms of grief and have grace for those who try and fail.

Below are some examples of what people might say to us, and why they might not be helpful. This is especially true in the early stages of grief. The *Self-Care Moment* that follows, explores more positive responses.

"At least they lived a good long life."
This dismisses your pain. You want them here, even if they are old. Your feelings of loss are valid, even if they lived a good, long life.

"You can always adopt another dog."
This trivializes your loss and the potential trauma of your experience. Arguably, all dogs can potentially create joy in our lives, but adopting another pet will not replace the relationship you had. Your grief is unique and deserves to be acknowledged and respected.

"Many dogs need to be adopted; another dog will make you feel better."
This implies that your loved one can be replaced, and again, this overlooks the unique bond you had. It also fails to acknowledge the depth of your loss and the time you need to heal.

"Let me know if there is anything I can do."
This is an empty promise, as there is nothing specific that can be done. What you need is for your pain to be witnessed and for others to be a life support for you while you float through grief and mourning.

"You have two other dogs; you need to find joy in them."
Again, I agree that all dogs can spark joy. You are grieving the loss of your dog, who died, and it's important to feel this loss in order to move towards remapping your connection with them.

"You need to get out and dance; let loose and shake it off."
This sends the message that your pain is unwelcome or should be

dismissed. This can be because people often feel uncomfortable with the expressions of grief, but it's important to honour your emotions by giving yourself space to feel in your own way. This may in fact be dancing, but only if this is what you decide is best for you.

"They are in a better place."
This one can be partially helpful, but no one knows for sure where they've gone, and even if we did know for sure, this does not bring them back. You really want them to be here with you, snuggling close like before.

"Everything happens for a reason."
Does it really? And if so, why did this happen to your dog under these circumstances? Such a thought might lead you to question if you somehow caused this or deserve this loss more than others, adding unnecessary blame.

"I know how you feel."
This statement comes from a place of trying to connect with you, but it can feel unhelpful because everyone's experience is different, and your dog is special to you.

"My dog died last year; let me tell you about what I did."
Again, this likely comes from a place of trying to help, but this kind of statement makes your loss about them. It probably doesn't feel supportive.

"Are you still feeling sad about this? Thought you'd be over it by now!"
People around us may feel uncomfortable when they cannot help us feel better, so they may try to point out how strong we are to feel helpful. Remember, there is no timeline for your grieving process.

"Be strong, be brave, keep your chin up — you are doing so well

today."
It's okay to have good days, as reinvesting in present life is the ultimate goal, but it's also okay to have sad days. Your grief must be witnessed and felt by you for it to be transformed. Doing so helps you adapt to living in the new world without your dog here.

"They were sick for so long; at least now you have closure."
Yes, there may be some relief now that your dog is no longer in pain or you no longer have the stress of caregiving, but you still wish they were here.

"This will end soon," or, "It will be over in a year."
Will it? We have no idea how long the emotional pain will last, and we certainly don't want to try and forget our loved one. Yes, it is generally accepted that as time passes, the pain subsides and growth occurs, but others must be careful not to suggest all will magically be as it was. Life will never be the same—but you will evolve and grow.

Self-Care Moment: What Do You Need to Hear?

Sometimes, even well-meaning people can say the most hurtful things to us during the grieving process! They think they are being comforting but they're not. We want to feel our big emotions around them without fear of being talked out of our pain.

This exercise will help you identify how you felt with unhelpful comments, and explore what you actually needed to hear. You will write multiple lists, so take your time to really assess what comes up. Remember to practice self-care as needed.

Scan the QR code to complete this Self-Care Moment:

The Story of Fudge: An Unexpected Transformation

A dog can offer us comfort and unconditional love. This is especially important if our caregivers do not do this for us during childhood. This was the case for the owner of Fudge, who had many family furry companions throughout childhood, who provided him with the feelings of safety and love.

Fudge's owner went about his adult life without a dog and remembers feeling disconnected from the world. One day, he was driving to a construction site when all of a sudden, he saw a little brown puppy on the side of the busy road. He stopped and scooped up the puppy, put it in his car, and drove around the area to see if anybody knew who the dog belonged to. He could not find the owner.

As he looked down at the small bundle of fur, he started to remember what the bond with a dog felt like. Then he sensed that this dog was for him, and realized that he was gifted with a puppy. This was exciting because he had never had a dog of his own, so he brought her home.

Welcoming Fudge into his house marked the beginning of a transformative journey, rekindling a sense of purpose and value for her owner. Fudge gave him a reason to come home and a companion to enjoy. After a month, Fudge's owner realized that having a dog had transformed his house into a home. Walking around the neighbourhood also opened opportunities to foster new friendships with neighbours, and Fudge was a real hit with the local children.

Tragically, during a playful moment with the neighbourhood kids, Fudge was accidentally let off her leash and was struck by a car. She passed away in her owner's arms.

Coping with the loss of Fudge was difficult, but her owner found comfort in remembering what Fudge had offered him during her precious life. He is sentimental regarding the sense of grounding she brought him, and is grateful for how she forever changed him for the better. Fudge was only in his life for about two years, but he feels she really helped him grow, and rescued him by taking him outside himself. Fudge's owner beams when he thinks about how she gave him a different connection with his community, and how she was his constant companion, even at work.

Fudge's owner believes in honouring the gifts of a dog by treasuring memories. He suggests recognizing the profound impact that dogs have on human lives, such as noticing a reason to be joyful each day. He wants others to know that saying goodbye to a beloved dog does not have to just be a farewell, but can also be a heartfelt expression of gratitude for the love and enriching experiences shared.

Turn Within: How did the bond with your dog help you feel connected with others?

Helping Children Understand Death

Anything that's human is mentionable, and anything that is mentionable can be more manageable. When we can talk about our feelings, they become less overwhelming, less upsetting, and less scary.
        —*Fred Rogers, Mr. Rogers' Neighbourhood*

One of the best personal examples I can share regarding speaking with children about death is when our cat died. My then 5-year-old daughter was very curious about what had happened to her. Kit had been a part of my daughter's life since she was born, and it was unusual for Kit not to be around. I explained, "Kit was in a lot of pain because she only had one back leg, and after many years like this, her back was making it hard for her to walk. We brought her to the vet, where they gave her some medicine to go into a deep sleep, then her body stopped breathing, and so she died. I believe that her soul is now in a heaven in the sky, where we will meet again one day."

Her eyes were full of wonder and terror at the same time. "Will I die in my sleep too?"

"No honey, Kit died because she was very sick. You are not sick."

After a pause, she asked, "But what happened to her body? It is still at the animal hospital?"

I replied, "Kit's body was cremated, where it was put into a special oven just for cremation, and it turned into ashes."

She nodded and continued colouring. I thought I had answered all of her questions and swept away any fears.

A few months later, my daughter and I were sitting in the waiting room of the dentist's office. I should notes that this child in particular, was a social butterfly and often sparked conversations with strangers. She walked up to a man in the waiting room, and he smiled at her.

She engaged with him, "Did you know that my cat, her name

is Kit? We loved her, but now we made her burning in the sun in the sky!" The man's jaw dropped, and I quickly inserted myself into the conversation to explain. It seemed I was not as clear as I had thought.

Dogs are a part of our family, and this means that our children will also need to deal with the loss of a canine loved one. Depending on the child's developmental stage, the impact of the loss can vary. How they respond depends on their cognitive development, how well they can manage their emotions, their level of communication skills, and their existing sense of security in the world. As we know, loss can also influence a future sense of security, identity, and relationships.

Validate Their Feelings & Monitor Behaviour Changes
Children may not fully understand the permanence of death, and so we need to help them navigate their grief. They are in the process of developing emotional regulation and emotional vocabulary, meaning, they are learning how to feel their feelings and how to use their words about them. Younger children might think death is temporary or reversible. Older children may be more developmentally ready to grasp the finality of death, but struggle with the emotional implications.

As children's brains are not yet fully developed, they do their best to make sense of their world. When they don't have all the information or when something is new and confusing, they fill in the blanks by extrapolating data— something really interesting that contributes to our creativity as humans. Unfortunately, this also means that children tend to resort to self-blame, or make connections around cause and effect based on fear.

For a child, death can be confusing and terrifying. Imagine wondering if death is contagious and not having the emotional vocabulary to ask about it. I have no doubt that when I told my daughter that Kit died because she was sick, the next time my daughter was sick it crossed her mind that she might go into a deep sleep and stop breathing as well. Or even worse, the next time I had the flu, she worried that I would l die! Consider what it would be like not to understand why everyone was acting so strange, and you kept getting into trouble by asking where the dog or cat was. It would be understandable to internalize and self-blame or shame.

Younger children may express their grief more through behaviour than through their words. They may regress, such as with toileting, have more frequent and intense tantrums, or withdraw. Although older children can express themselves better verbally, they may also show their grief through behaviour, academics, or peer relationships. Children tend to grieve in short bursts, alternating between being in a state of normal play and of sadness. Grief may also present itself in children as tummy aches, headaches, or other physical complaints.

It is important that we see these changes as expressions of grief, where the child needs comfort and reassurance, and not as defiance or behaviour that needs reprimand. They need us to interpret their behaviours and respond with understanding so they can learn to understand what they are feeling and what to do with it. If we are patient and flexible, we can recognize that they do not have the words to articulate their grief, and we can offer them the support they need.

We can say, "Feeling sad, angry, or confused is okay. Everyone feels different things when someone we love dies. You might feel sad for a long time, and that's normal, or you might not know what you are feeling."

We can encourage expression by saying, "Do you want to talk about how you're feeling? Would you like to draw a picture of your feelings or of a memory with Daisey?" By the way, if they choose to draw a gruesome scene of death, this is an amazing opportunity to ask open-ended questions so they can fully process their feelings, "Tell me more about what is happening in this picture." After we've validated their feelings and compassionately clarified any untrue thoughts, we can invite them to join us in drawing a more joyful memory. If they decline, that's okay too.

When we acknowledge their feelings, we're sending a message that it is normal to feel a range of emotions, such as sadness, anger, confusion, and even relief. It is helpful to allow them to express their emotions through talking, drawing, playing, or other activities they enjoy.

Offer Reassurance, Stability, Patience, & Understanding
Keeping routines as consistent as possible provides a stable and predictable environment. Physical comforts such as hugs and cuddles can be very comforting for children, offering a sense of normalcy and security.

Although a child may wish to console us from our sadness, it is key that we offer them comfort for their benefit, not ours. It is appropriate for children to see us cry, but it is not appropriate for them to feel alone with their feelings or to feel as though they must be responsible for emotionally supporting adults.

Children watch our every move, analyze their environment as best they can, and copy what they see. One of the best things we can do is model healthy grieving and offer them guidance on how to express their emotions. By using simple language and reassuring them about their own safety and the safety of others, children can move through grief in a healthy and constructive way.

We can offer, "Even though Daisey's body is no longer with us, we can still remember. We can talk about our happy times together or anything you'd like. I'll be here to help you answer any questions you have."

Honest Communication & Educate Them About Grief
Children expect us to tell them the truth. As they are so literal, they need us to guide them through their emotional truth.

By explaining death with age-appropriate terms and avoiding euphemisms, we can reduce fear. Saying they "died" instead of "passed away" offers clarity. We can say, "I'm very sad to tell you that Daisey has died. Dying means that her body has stopped working, and she can't live. She will not be coming back."

Encouraging children to ask questions and showing that we can answer them truthfully, reinforces safety and sends the message that it's okay to have big feelings. It also sends the message that not having big feelings is fine, and that whatever is happening for them is okay.

As children are so literal, it is essential that if we don't know the answer, we say so. It's alright to say what we believe and to ask them what they believe in, keeping the conversation open and honest. We cannot promise them that we or they will never die, because this is not true. We can offer them reassurance of what we can control regarding health, and living a fulfilling life.

We can let them know that grief feels different every day and comes like waves. It is key to let them know they have our ongoing support and show them that it's okay to grieve. We are their lifeline, their ship on the ocean through the storm. We do this by modelling healthy ways to cope with loss.

We don't need to have these difficult conversations all on our own! There are many children's books about grief that can help explain death and feelings in a gentle and accessible way. There are also bereavement organizations that offer children appropriate resources for coping with grief through videos, activities, and worksheets.

Involve Them in Rituals & Encourage Remembering
As part of their support system, we can absolutely include children in rituals and memorials to help them feel connected and a sense of closure. We can draw pictures with them, share our favourite stories, and let them know they are not alone in grief. They can be encouraged to create their own ways to remember their loved one: planting a tree, making a scrapbook, creating a memory box, or writing a poem may be a good fit.

We can include them by offering, "Would you like to choose some pictures of Daisey to put in a picture frame in living room?" or "We can make a memory box of things that remind us of her." or "Would you like to help me hang the special Christmas ornament for Daisey?"

Children can be allowed to be a part of the euthanasia process or memorial services if they wish. The key is age-appropriate decisions and consent. We can assist them with their decision by explaining what will happen and what they can expect. We must also be realistic about what to expect from them. Although younger children do benefit from rituals and mourning, it is unrealistic to expect a young child to sit quietly during a celebration of a life ceremony, as they just don't have the mental and physical capacity to do so. As well, a younger child will not understand the process of euthanasia, and so they may require more support during the appointment.

Consider if perhaps it isn't beneficial for them to be present, or if they may take away from your ability to be present in the last moments of your dog's life. It is most important that, if possible, our dog's last moments are calm. There may be more age-friendly ways for children to join us in rituals and remembering.

Seek Professional Support

Although a child may be expressing grief in a healthy way through behaviours that may be considered regression or difficult, we should also be on alert for red flags. Changes in behaviour, sleep, appetite, or school performance can also be signs that a child is struggling and needs additional support. Without making the subject a topic which will suggest something is wrong with them, we can check in with them regularly to assess how they are coping over time.

We can ask, "When you think of Daisey now, what comes up for you?", or, "What do you think is your favourite memory of Daisey?"

Just as for us, when children grow and move through developmental stages, grief may resurface. We can support them by being open to revisiting conversations about their loss, and we can offer them additional support such as through play therapy to express grief and process their emotions.

Unhelpful Statements

Avoiding the truth, invalidating emotions, discouraging expression, making comparisons, and providing false reassurance are all mistakes we might make when trying to console a grieving child. The following are some examples of unhelpful comments, and some alternative suggestions:

"Daisey has gone to sleep and won't wake up."
"We lost Daisey."
This is not accurate or honest.

Instead, try describing what has happened and why they are not coming back alive:
"Daisey's body has died, which means she ahs stopped breathing and is no longer alive. She will not be coming home, but we will always remember her in our hearts."

"You shouldn't cry, Daisey wouldn't want you to be sad."
"Be strong, there's no need to be upset."
"Don't think about it too much."
"Let's not talk about it; it just makes you sad."
"Don't be sad; we'll see them again someday."
This response is dismissive of the very feelings all humans must feel to process grief in a healthy way!

Instead, try validating their feelings regardless of how big or small. Offer compassion and openness. Here's an example:
"I can see you are crying and feeling sad that Daisey has died. Would you like a hug? I will also miss her, especially how she used to snuggle with us on the couch."

"Everything will be back to normal soon."
This sends the message that nothing has changed, and to a child's small world a lot has changed—forever.

Instead, try validating this change and offering guidance that the pain that comes with grief is for a purpose:

"It sure feels quiet and empty when we come home now. No one was as excited to see us as Daisey when we'd come through the door! I think we will always miss her big hello kisses, because we will always love her. Today out heart hurts, but one day, our heart will remember the happiness of her kisses more than the sadness of missing her."

"At least we still have our other dog."

"Other kids have lost more, and you're lucky it was just your dog."

It is important to send the message that no one can replace our child's sibling/friend, and their relationship mattered.

We can offer:

"Daisey was a very special dog, and I know you love her very much."

Additional Tips

Letting a child guide how much or how little they want to talk about their loss, models respect for boundaries and feelings. Offer information in small, age-appropriate doses, and expect that they will ask the same questions multiple times. They are trying to understand the concept of death and permanence, something their brain may not be developmentally ready for yet.

Model healthy grieving. Show them that it's okay to be sad and to grieve. Help them to understand their feelings are a normal part of life, and let them know that missing their dog will be forever, but the sadness that comes with loss, is not.

Helping Dogs Understand Death

Dogs are part of the family and also have an attachment to other dogs in the home. One of the questions we had in my home was if we should invite Hero and Nilla in the room when Aura passed away. We made the decision to have them present throughout, and have the opportunity to smell her afterward. I believe this was the right decision for them.

Hero is a rescue dog from the streets in the Bahamas. Even though he was just a puppy when we adopted him, I have no doubt that in his earlier life he was exposed to loss. I imagine that either through an injury in the pack, or the need to eat, he understood death before he started his life with us. Right after Aura died, Hero walked over to smell Aura; then his eyes bulged before promptly relocating himself to the corner of the room. He understood.

Nilla, on the other hand, was new to the idea of death. I think she was aware that something upsetting was happening with us, and she was more than happy to come to our emotional aid on the kitchen floor that afternoon. It wasn't until later that we noticed she was walking from room to room, seemingly searching for something.

Both Hero and Nilla experienced a period of time lying down extra quiet after Aura's death. Although they could not speak, I believe they were grieving. I offered extra snuggles to remind them it was going to be okay.

CHAPTER FOUR: *THE LEGACY OF A DOG'S LOVE*

Banana & Lemon

For months after Aura passed away, there was a void in the house and in my heart. The pain was unbearable! *She was just a dog*, I tried to tell myself. I needed to get over it and move on with my life. After all, I had my two other dogs, Nilla and Hero, a loving family, and overall a good life.

I felt like I lost someone who was between my child and a soul mate. I'd go through waves of shame about my sadness; I felt alone, like no one understood. I could not move forward. I was having flashes of Aura wandering the halls, and of her lifeless body in my arms. The intrusive thought of *I killed her* haunted me. I tried to fill my painful void with overworking, chocolate chips, and that extra glass of wine I didn't need. When this approach didn't work, I wondered if another dog would fix my heart. Not to replace Aura, but to help fill the void.

My husband and I agreed to foster again. A Pug named Banana then entered our life, a lovely soul who was suffering from five massive bladder stones. She had the softest fur that was a deep apricot colour. As her nose snares were nearly fully closed, each breath was a loud grunt from the back of her throat. She was in so uncomfortable that every breath sounded like a struggle for her, and she was painfully peeing blood every few minutes.

Banana lived with us for over a month while we cared for her medical needs. As she was incontinent, we mostly kept her company in a separate space while we waited for her medicine to start working so she could have a surgery. In spite of her pain and loud breathing, she was so happy to be with us, especially when she was allowed to join the whole pack for TV time every night. Her favourite spot was the back of the couch—her sunshine bliss equivalent—folded up ducky style while lovingly mouthing a tennis ball.

As Banana's primary caregiver, she and I grew closer. As if my heart started to enlarge, I noticed that I began to heal. Banana was not a replacement for Aura; the void she left was still there, but I seemed to have more space and tolerance for a new connection. There was a unique yet familiar colour of love starting to form between Banana and me. When I'd come into the room, she'd light up and radiate an amazing energy, saying, "I'm so glad you are here." Tapping into my emotions, I started to feel safe again, and my husband was sharing in her love too. We were considering adopting Banana after her recovery, but we needed more time. I knew her lengthy recovery would give us this.

On the day of Banana's surgery, we dropped her off at the vet. Gave her kisses and said we'd see her later. The drop-off was quick because at the time, everyone had limited contact protocols to stop the spread of COVID-19. The foster manager was going to call us when it was time to pick her up, so we went on about our day, knowing it would be a couple of hours. A couple of hours turned into many hours, and I'll never forget the call when it finally came.

"They are still working on her; something isn't going right. It seems like her intestines are fused together or something. I'll call you back when I have more information."

Later that night, the foster manager called us back and gave us the news that the surgery unsuccessful and that Banana would likely die that evening. We were given the choice for Banana to come to our place to pass away, or for her to stay with him. He told us that one of his dogs had been known in the past to comfort palliative dogs, and this sounded like the right choice for Banana.

That night, we went to bed knowing that Banana would pass away peacefully medicated in her sleep, snuggled up with warm furry companion to guide her over the rainbow. Because this happened during the COVID-19 pandemic, saying our final goodbye in person was not an option. My goodbye at the vet of "I'll see you later", still stand true.

My grief rolled in harder than ever. Life felt hard, cruel, and unfair. My heart was raw, and I was not functioning well inside. I decided to seek therapy and began to finally process my trauma and grief—all of it. It all counted because it was all connected: being bullied in elementary school, losing my grandpa, bad teen choices, bad adult choices, legal co-parenting stuff, teacher phone calls, awkward university social situations, and dog loss. Thanks to my therapist, much soul searching and many tears, I was able to finally set most of it free within a year.

Then Limoncello (Lemon) joined our family, a mini pug with a big attitude who had clearly imprinted her love on me. I thought I was ready, but five months after her adoption, I was still missing Aura every time I looked at Lemon. I felt terrible because Lemon adored me, but I just couldn't return the same level of love and connection that she was offering. I wondered if I had made a mistake by adopting her.

It was Christmas, and the nostalgic music in the kitchen moved me to dance. I cradled my tiny puppy in my arms as I gently rocked back and forth to the beat. Staring out the window at the frozen patio where Aura used to sunbathe, past Christmas memories with Aura suddenly flooded me.

At first, I cried with sadness. Then the thought of how wonderful it was that Aura and I grew together over the years came to mind. Even when life was feeling good, she made life feel better. My mind flashed through memories of our time together—the day I brought her home and how my children bleated with joy, the day I couldn't concentrate on my schoolwork because she was snoring so loud, her sneaking into the bed at 4 a.m. for snuggles, the moments she soothed my crying soul because it wasn't my day with my children, and the silence we enjoyed together in the backyard.

Suddenly, I could feel Aura's love in my chest. It was a warm, swirling sensation, and I cried with joy and gratitude. I missed her love so much. As I looked down and kissed the sleeping puppy in my arms, I permitted myself to feel her love as well. I continued rocking back and forth with her as I held her closer, and visualized allowing the warmth from my chest to hug Lemon.

Just then, my husband walked into the room. Instinctively, he hugged me and asked if I was missing Aura. I nodded yes, and after a loving kiss on the forehead, he quietly left me to continue processing.

I had finally let go of what I no longer needed—pain and self-blame. I accepted that I was not required to remember Aura in terror in order to honour her. I stopped questioning if I made the right choice, or if I made the right choice fast enough. I realized that I'll love Aura forever, so I'll miss her forever, and that's okay. I became aware that I get to keep all our memories and how she made me feel. She helped teach me to love myself again. I felt permission to accept the love of the puppy in my arms.

Aura showed me that love has many colours, and that giving and receiving a rainbow of love can be safe. I get to keep that, and I choose to let go of the rest.

Memories Are the Bridge

I believe that from the time we start to grow, everything that happens to us and around us shapes how we experience the world. The messages we receive through our mother's hormones, sounds while in the womb, and then later through actual interactions help us learn what it means to exist and how we can respond to different situations. Each new experience adds to our existing memory networks, influencing our worldview and our emotional reactions.

Our minds have a natural way of processing experiences and emotions, which helps us learn and grow. Sometimes, when we encounter difficult events like the loss of a loved one, our natural processing of events can become overwhelmed, making it harder to cope with our emotions.

When we remember certain moments of our dog, such as seeing or feeling their lifeless body, it's normal to feel disturbed or upset by these thoughts. This is especially true in the first six to nine months after the loss. Over time, the intensity of our feelings usually lessens. This is because, as we have multiple new experiences, we begin to reorient ourselves within our new world without them. If we don't start to feel a shift, we might be stuck in our grief, or we might have trauma and need some extra help.

Memories act as a bridge between the world before and the new world without our dog. Even though memories of our dog make us miss them and can bring up painful emotions, memories also hold the key to our healing journey.

This is because we all hold an inner representation of our loved ones based on our experiences with them. The inner representation of our dog needs updating.

If memories are what bridge our past experiences to our present reality, then positive memories are what help us connect and find meaning within our grief. When we access positive memories, this can help counteract past negative experiences, offering us healing and resilience. While our intense pain may make it temporarily difficult to access our positive memories, these memories patiently wait to be reactivated.

If accessing memories are the essential building blocks of how we represent our loved one inside us, then actively engaging with memories in the present time—especially the positive ones—is the path to healing.

It is important that we remain in the present, so our system does not get confused about the timeline. Reliving our trauma is not helpful. Remaining time-oriented and remembering our dog as if watching the past like a movie, helps our system to assimilate their love into our new world. We know it happened to us, but the moment of death has passed. Time, has passed. By acknowledging and validating all memories and their truths, we can begin to rediscover our new connection with our dog, and find a sense of peace.

Sometimes we may need a little help accessing the important aspects of our memories. This is because the emotional pain of grief blocks the existing positive neural networks that are already stored within us. When the pain finally subsides—and the clouds part for the sun to shine again—we regain capacity to access these positive neural networks. This is when adaptive information is assimilated, and our grief beings to transform our inner representation of our loved one. Experiencing the full spectrum of emotions of our grief is an essential part of this chain reaction. This is also when our system purges what we no longer need—the trauma, self-blame, and shame—and allows us to exist in the new world while accessing the joyful life we had with our dog.

We want to work toward remembering them with mostly the positive stuff at the forefront, because this is what is true and helpful to live our life. Through practices like strengthen vagal tone, acknowledging personal mastery, and regular gratitude explained in this book, we can help our system access and tolerate our positive and more helpful memories. EMDR therapy can also help by expediting this process.

Grief is not a disease, and moving forward is possible. We all have the resilience within us to navigate our grief.

The Story of Orbit: Legacy of Group Hugs

Orbit was a charming Irish setter mix who holds a special place in her family's hearts. She was by their side through thick and thin, taking part in fun and challenging times. Even when faced with skunks, porcupine quills, and her playful antics, Orbit remained a cherished companion in the family.

Whenever someone called out "group hug," they would all gather on the bed for a cozy snuggle. The tradition of the "group hug" with Orbit was more than just a playful routine; it became a symbol of love, comfort, and togetherness in their family.

Orbit, with her lively and affectionate nature, eagerly participated in these group hugs, bouncing into bed with excitement whenever they called out the familiar words. Each "group hug" session was a moment of pure joy and connection.

When Orbit died, her family was devastated. Despite the distractions of daily life, the emptiness they felt lasted for months. Their grief eventually found a path through an unexpected source; a white and beige Samoyed mix named Alpine.

Keeping Orbit's spirit of love and togetherness alive in their home, the family was talking about teaching Alpine "group hug". As they were discussing how to teach him this, Alpine jumped on the bed as if he knew exactly what to do! His excitement mirrored Orbit's and it was as if Orbit's spirit was guiding Alpine, teaching him the importance of love and togetherness within their family.

As they continued to share these moments with Alpine, the family felt a sense of healing and renewal. The "group hugs" became a bridge between past memories with Orbit and new relationships, including Alpine. It was a testament to the legacy of love that Orbit had left behind.

The family feels Alpine's natural understanding of a group hug is a reminder that Orbit's spirit lives on in the moments they share with Alpine.

Turn Within: What was a unique quirk about your dog?

Self-Care Moment: Happiness Files

I call this activity *Happiness Files* because it is all about helping our system remember what it's like to focus on accessing positive feelings and sensations. The more we encourage our brain to do this, the easier it gets. This also supports our brain to access the much needed sense of connection to our loved one.

1. Create a folder that you can easily access on your phone or computer.
2. Include photos, video, and audio of happy memories across your lifespan, or that simply spark joy. Some examples include:
   - Pleasant images you find online
   - Short videos with soothing sounds of nature
   - Favourite guided meditations
   - Photos of favourite memories
3. Come back to this folder often, especially if you are having a sad day. Notice the pleasant shift inside you as your brain invites your neurons to fire and rewire.

Scan the QR code to complete this Self-Care Moment:

Is Pain Necessary?

Some women in labour use the mantra that the pain has a purpose. As long as they remember this, they know the pain will not last forever and that it is required for what is to come next. Thankfully, after each child is born our brain instantly knows that the memory of the physical pain is no longer needed, and so it purges this information. I suspect that holding a new baby alongside a rush of oxytocin helps with this process.

Unfortunately, the brain is a little slower to rewire and purge the pain regarding grief. Grief can sometimes feel like a phantom limb, where our mind creates a space where our loved one still exists physically here, even though we know they are gone. It is normal and natural to always miss our dog, because our love for them will never fade.

Here's the good news: although feelings of sadness are required as a catalyst to reorient and remap us in our new world, our pain is not necessary to keep loving and honouring our loved one after our brain has remapped.

This may sound counterintuitive, and we might even believe that if we let go of the pain, we will somehow forget our dog. The truth is, we will never forget our dog. We will always hold their love within us because this love is embedded there, and nothing can take this from us.

As discussed earlier, when we were younger, we instinctively stayed in close proximity to our caregivers because they were what we hoped would keep us alive and healthy. At times our attachment system might have felt threatened, such as our mom letting an extended family member hold us while she left the room. As a way to protect us, our system would have signaled yearning and pain within us to motivate us to fix the situation and get Mom back to us. Most likely, this would have manifested in us crying in loud protest!

The pain associated with our grief comes from the deep attachment to our dog. With our loss, our system is reacting the same way, except there is no possibility of maintaining physical closeness to make it feel safer. The pain with grief is meant to guide us to feeling safe and secure again, and our system is desperately trying to find a way to do the impossible—to reconnect physically with our loved one. But when our mind finally realizes that the pain is guiding us to seek something that is no attainable, it can conclude that it needs to find another way to cope with this perceived void. Through the grieving process, our brain will eventually reinvest its energy into remapping our connection with our loved one.

It's natural to fear that letting go of our grief means letting go of our connection to our dog. The fact that they are no longer physically with us is confusing for our brain at first, making it a challenge to know how to move forward without feeling immense pain. When we grieve, we are holding onto an internal image and meaning of our loved one as they were when they were alive. However, they are no longer physically present, and this creates a disconnect in our minds, like a glitch in a computer program. Our system grapples with assimilating the loss and adjusting to a world without their physical presence, which is incredibly painful. The only way to get through is to rewire and reprogram because the current program is no longer working!

It's important to recognize that attachments are transformed, not lost. Over time, our dog's inner representation will evolve, meaning we will eventually be able to comprehend and hold the truth that they are no longer alive or physically present, yet we can find new ways to feel connected to them. This transformation requires pain, but the end result does not require us to hold onto the pain. Rather, the grieving process will enable us to carry their essence within us in a meaningful and evolved way.

One way to navigate grief and let go of the pain is to actively find ways to stay connected with the deceased. Keeping their memory close by and remembering their legacy through rituals, conversations, or special traditions can serve as a comforting bridge to our healing. Remembering our past connections reminds us of the love and impact they had on our lives, and helps us ride through the storm waves of grief. With each wave, we gradually regain full access to our positive memories, while holding the truth that they are no longer physically here.

The grief we feel is an echo of the bond we have for our dog. As humans, we are incredibly resilient and able to endure this element of love. Their life mattered, and their legacy lives within us.

The Story of Cinder and Joey: Embracing the Joy

Cinder, as shown in the left photo above, was a dog that was supposed to be just for the wife of a couple. Instead, Cinder mutually fell in love with her husband leading to their unexpected relationship of unconditional love and dedicated loyalty. Cinder loved to lay on the pool deck and was a big snuggler. When excited, Cinder would spin and spin, causing drool to cover the room!

Cinder's mom went to the pound to adopt another dog just for her, and to complete their family. The instant her eyes met with Joey, a Dalmatian, she didn't need to see any other dogs, as she knew they were meant for each other. Although the vet said that Joey had likely been stabbed, this did not stop her from loving him or him from enjoying his new life.

This was especially evident when he ran in the yard; Joey would beam as he raced around in his newfound freedom. His owner describes this memory as witnessing pure joy.

A funny memory of Cinder and Joey is about a day when their mom had both dogs on leashes for a walk. Cinder was doing her business as usual when she accidentally pooped on the leash. Then, Cinder moved quickly, wrapping the leash around her owner's legs, getting poop on her. As the owner was trying to untangle herself, the Joey did the exact same thing by pooping nearby, then getting distracted by an animal and running in circles. Their owner found herself tangled in poopy leashes, unable to move! By the time she got home, she and the dogs were entirely covered in poop! The only thing she could do was laugh.

Joey was eventually diagnosed with Cushing's disease, and the medication had terrible side effects. His owner tried other options to ease his pain, such as herbal medicines, but his decline continued. Joey got to the point where he couldn't walk or go to the bathroom on his own, and a decision was made out of his owner's love for him.

Her belief is that "when dogs can't do what brings them joy and happiness, that's not living a doggy life." His owner described feeling like Joey had been created just for her, and so his loss felt like a piece of her soul had been ripped away, akin to losing a child.

Years later, she and her husband adopted a new puppy, joining Cinder and completing their family again. Shortly after, Cinder had a severe seizure in the middle of the night and died instantly. The owner explained that they found softness within their grief when hugging their new puppy.

Cinder and Joey's mom believes that an explanation for why humans often outlive their dogs is that dogs have so much love that they don't need to live so long. They are quicker to forgive and can recognize that not all people are bad. Their lives are short because they're pure—everything is an invitation to play and enjoy life.

Her advice to others is to go hug a puppy. She feels this will heal a broken heart and that our dog would want us to do this. As well she found learning to ride the waves of the pain and letting it wash over her, helped her come through her grief. She knew that if she could let herself feel it, she would get through it. She believes that if we welcome the pain as a pain with purpose, we can be reassured we will be okay.

She thinks it's important to make an effort to remember the silly and fun times. The fun memories of drool, poop, and pure joy help her to keep Cinders' and Joeys' memories close to her heart, right where they belong.

Turn Within: What is your favourite funny memory?

Self-Care Moment: Tapping Into Love

This activity shows that love never goes away, even After-Death. It's focused on helping you reconnect with your deceased loved one by thinking of a favourite memory of them that sparks joy. You can do this activity regarding your dog, or another deceased loved one.

Use this tool to honour and celebrate the bond you shared with your loved one, keeping their memory alive in your heart and mind. By actively engaging with the feelings of love, you can start to reexperience a sense of connection, even in their physical absence. *Practice Tapping into Love* regularly to nurture your new relationship with them.

Listen to the guided meditation here:

Three Phases of Mourning

Grief is a real, heartfelt reaction to the end of someone's meaningful life. It's not a straightforward process but rather a journey filled with ups and downs. At times, we will feel the loss, such as when we cry or while visiting their grave, and there will be times when we move toward restoration, like when we can enjoy going to the movies or engaging in other activities. It's essential that we oscillate between these states of mourning and rejuvenation in order to manage the intensity of our grief, and to cope in healthy ways.

There are unwritten rules about where and how we can show our grief, usually favouring keeping our grief private and keeping it within certain boundaries. Sometimes, we feel pressured to appear strong and keep our emotions to ourselves, especially since society often praises resilience—particularly when it comes to the loss of a pet. However, grief isn't just about emotions; it can also affect us physically, making it even harder to move through the dark storm.

Many of us might be familiar with the stages of grief identified by Elizabeth Kübler-Ross:

The five emotions she highlighted were:
1. Denial
2. Anger
3. Bargaining
4. Depression
5. Acceptance

That model was created to describe the stages of grief when someone is diagnosed with a terminal illness, and don't always apply for our situation. This does not mean she was incorrect; the five stages of grief were not meant to be used as a general model for all grief.

Therese Rando speaks of Three Phases of Mourning, which

might be a better model for a broader range of grief. This model is fluid, and we can sometimes be in more than one phase at the same time. Rando suggests that we are in complicated mourning if we get stuck in any of the Three Phases of Mourning:

1. Avoidance

The Avoidance phase is characterized by a sense of confusion and shock, where the mind struggles to grasp the reality of our loss. Here, we must recognize our loss and the reality of death, even if it initially feels surreal or incomprehensible. We are in this phase when we are attempting to comprehend the fact of death and the consequences. It's common to feel numb and detached, or we might engage in behaviours that distract us from facing the full weight of our loss. This phase is essentially a protective mechanism, so our mind can gradually come to terms with our new reality without being overwhelmed by our emotions.

2. Confrontation

As time progresses, the Confrontation phase emerges, where we finally begin to react to the separation. This is when the emotional impact of our loss becomes more pronounced. Here, we allow ourselves to experience and express the range of emotions that accompany our grief, including sadness, anger, guilt, and longing.

This phase is a period of facing our pain head-on, acknowledging the depth of our loss, and beginning to process our emotions. Our grief will come and go as we assimilate and adapt to our new world. Here, we reflect on and cherish the memories shared with our dog. This is painful, but we eventually find solace and meaning in the moments spent with them.

This phase is important; it helps us evolve by understanding the impacts of our loss, allowing us to adapt and understand how to exist in the new world. Our memories act as a bridge between the world before they died and the current new world without them here. Our mind and body act together, purging what we no longer need by letting go of expectations, roles, and unnecessary attachments tied to our dog.

Knowing that all memories of our dog are the building blocks of the image we hold inside us—our inner representation—we can trust that our attachment system is rewiring and reprogramming so we can exist in equilibrium again.

3. Accommodation

The final phase, Accommodation, marks a turning point where acceptance and adaptation really begin to take shape. Acceptance doesn't mean forgetting or moving on from our loss; it involves integrating the reality of our dog's absence into our daily life. This phase is about adjusting to the changes and discovering ways to honour our dog's memory while living a fulfilling life.

We have reached this phase when we can interact with the current world adaptively and functionally without fear of forgetting the old world. At this point, we can exist in life while also experiencing satisfaction in living. We will easily remember our dog without the intrusive and negative images, and we can access the positive memories easily. The sad stuff will still be there, but it won't feel like it is right in our face and forcing us to reexperience big waves of feelings.

When we are in the Accommodation phase, we can redirect and focus our energy on meaningful activities, relationships, and goals, and find joy and purpose in life despite our loss.

Everyone's bereavement process is unique because their connection with their loss is unique to them. The circumstances of the death and our psychological and biological makeup influence our unique bereavement experience. There is no one correct way to process loss or receive treatment. It's important to recognize that grief is a nonlinear process, and we may find ourselves moving back and forth between phases, and that's okay!

Our goal isn't to "get over" our loss. Instead, we aim to find ways to carry the love and memories of our deceased loved one in the present, while continuing to build a meaningful and resilient life.

Healing and growth are possible. We usually cannot do this alone, as may need support from loved ones or professionals. We also need to have a willingness to embrace the complexity of our grief through self-compassion, and time.

The Story of Coco: Rescued by Love

The story of Coco, a rescue dog at the age of 12, illuminates how freedom and solace can begin for us at any age.

Despite Coco's physical challenges of being blind and deaf, his owner was drawn to his one-eyed face through a photo online. She felt an instant connection that spoke to her heart. "I don't have the words to describe that ball of love and hope. He was just pure joy."

During a difficult time in her relationship with her partner, Coco's role as a faithful companion took on a deeper significance. As Coco offered a sense of stability, loyalty, and light, his owner found hope. Coco's unconditional love served as a constant beacon of support, helping his owner cope with her emotions and keeping her grounded. She found a renewed sense of resilience, and was able to navigate the challenges of family breakdown.

After three years of living his new life, Coco's health quickly began to decline with seizures. He spent his last twenty-four hours in his owner's arms, cradled with love and tenderness as he peacefully passed away. His owner faced the pain of letting go, but found peace in being there for Coco, knowing that Coco's last moments were surrounded by love.

The loss of Coco was undeniably heartbreaking. His owner feels their relationship served as a catalyst for positive change, clarity, and growth. She was able to transform her grief into action by reassessing the people and priorities in her life, and making decisions that led to a more fulfilling existence.

Through this journey, Coco's legacy lives on as a reminder of the profound impact that pets have on our emotional well-being, and the enduring bond that transcends time and space.

Turn Within: Bring up a time when your dog was a beacon of light for you. Notice where and how you feel that loving connection in your body.

Self-Care Moment: Complicated Grief

The questionnaire for this exercise is designed to help you assess whether you might be in complicated grief, meaning, stuck in the Three Phases of Mourning. It is not diagnostic, but it helps give an idea of whether it's time to reach out for professional support.

It is provided by The Hospice Support Fund, and the original version with a deeper explanation of it can be accessed through the link shown on this *Self-Care Moment*.

Scan the QR code to complete this Self-Care Moment:

CHAPTER FIVE: *SPACE, TIME &*
ATTACHMENT

Honouring Aura's Memory

After Aura passed, I realized I didn't have many photos of her closer to right before she crossed over the rainbow. To be fully honest, at first, I was okay with that because any photo of her washed grief over me, leaving me sitting in a deep puddle of sadness. I put Aura's collar in a drawer, and in the early phase of my grief, I'd occasionally open the drawer but couldn't bring myself even to touch it. I would try, but it was as if a forcefield were stopping me. Looking back, I think this was because part of me thought that somehow, feeling her collar would make it real that she was gone.

As I moved through my grief, I was able to visit her collar more often. I know it sounds silly to say out loud that touching and visiting my deceased dog's collar was an accomplishment, but for me, this was a milestone. When I finally picked it up, memories of her soft fur, pug snorts, and how she was such a wise soul came flooding back to me. Eventually, I started to enjoy this ritual.

I honour my relationship with Aura in other ways as well. I have a Christmas ornament of a black pug that I hang on my tree every year. I take that moment to say thank you to her for all the love, gifts, and growth she shared with me. As well, Tom Grantis is an artist who drew a portrait of Aura. An image of his illustration is below, and you might recognize it from the cover this book. It is framed on my fireplace mantle, alongside other family photos. Every time I see it, it makes me smile.

Sunshine & Tennis Balls

One day, my younger son and I were walking our dogs, and all of a sudden, he said, "I still miss Aura. I make sure to remember her with the fun we had because it feels good. I also believe that as long as I remember her, it helps her have fun and to remember us—wherever happens next." I felt a chill track down my arms. For some reason, I thought that I was the only one still missing her. I could not take his grief away, but I was comforted that he was in a much better place than I was at the time.

None of us have definite proof of what happens after we die. If he finds solace in the idea that his loving thoughts can send positive energy to Aura, creating a joyful afterlife experience for her, and if this brings comfort to his grieving process without causing harm or stress, then I support him in remembering happy memories with Aura. It's a way of honouring her memory, and expressing his love.

Personally, imagining Aura and Banana running joyfully with other dogs in a serene meadow brings me comfort. I can envision them as healthy, active, and content. Sometimes, I picture Aura basking in the sunlight on a flat rock near a waterfall. She is fully healthy with two eyes, and she seems younger with shiny black fur. I imagine Banana happily playing nearby in the shade with a small tennis ball, breathing easily and pain-free.

These images help me cope with my loss and maintain a connection with them. With this image, I can keep their memories alive in a positive way. I have also incorporated my son's idea that when I send them loving energy, they benefit from it.

Turn Within: Are there others who also felt the love and loss of your dog?

Getting Unstuck

We don't move on. We move through our grief. One of the most painful things I experienced was when others, trying to act out of kindness, would suggest I move on. That wasn't helpful, as their comment suggested that Aura was a thing that could be replaced, and that her life and her love for me didn't matter. Grief was not a choice, and I was doing everything possible to heal! Getting over her was not a choice.

My early stages of grief were blocking my ability to feel connected to Aura, and this was a perpetual pain. I wanted to remember the happy moments, but all my mind could focus on was the trauma and emptiness I felt. I was stuck, and I needed to find a way to move through my grief. As an EMDR therapist, I knew that EMDR could be helpful, so I worked with a therapist who offered this instrumental therapy to help me become unstuck.

I will never be okay that Aura is no longer with me, but as of now, the movie of her death no longer feels intrusive when I bring her to mind. I have come to a point where the memory of her agreeing to adopt me, her sleeping in the sunshine, and the life gifts she gave me feel strong and make me smile inside. There was a time when I truly believed that I had failed her and that she judged me for my decisions. Now, I genuinely believe she remembers a good life with me, and I can feel reconnected to her love.

As I write this book, Aura has been gone for almost four years. I haven't moved on— I've moved through. I will always miss her because she will always be deceased. Also true, is that I will always love her and she will never be forgotten.

I now have three dogs, and I love them all while experiencing a different colour of love with each dog. They did not replace Aura. My heart grew bigger, and the space that she filled when she was here is full again with new meaning. My love for Aura will never die, and I can sense that she and I are forever connected. The pain of missing her is not something I need on order to keep our connection alive.

What Do Others Do?

Many of us rely on various coping mechanisms and strategies to cope with grief, often drawing on personal preferences, cultural practices, and individual beliefs. For example, I like to go for a walk in nature, exercise, look through old photos, or absorb some puppy love directly from one of my dogs at home.

Some of us turn to music as it has a powerful ability to help us feel our emotions, and provides us with a channel for processing feelings. Many music apps now have playlists already made with upbeat and empowering songs—maybe take some time to listen now.

Humour and laughter can offer us moments of relief and

shared connection. Making space for comedy amidst sadness can be a way to bond with others, and alleviate some of the heaviness of our grief. Humour helps us to reframe and redefine our problems. We also know that when we laugh, our body is not in a state of stress—something we can all benefit from more often. Watch a movie, get tickets for a stand-up comedy show, look through photos, or share memories of the fun times.

We all need a space to feel heard, seen, and valued, and talking to others about our grief can be incredibly therapeutic. We can share memories of our dog, discuss feelings of our loss, and accept receiving empathy from friends and family. Some people find that seeking professional support through therapy or joining a bereavement support group can be helpful in navigating grief. Make a date to have lunch with a support person—or reach out to a therapist. Schedule this on the calendar now!

Engaging in rituals or ceremonies for the deceased is another way that we can honour and remember our loved one. This may look like creating a memorial with photographs or meaningful objects, wearing clothing that symbolizes mourning or renewal, or participating in cultural or religious practices that offer comfort and connection.

Additionally, activities such as journaling, physical exercise, or exploring spirituality can offer avenues for healthy and constructive processing and healing.

If we find ourselves leaning towards avoiding our grief by suppressing or always containing our emotions, we have to remember that allowing ourselves to cry and experience the full range of emotions is a natural, and important part of the grieving process. This is not a weakness; feeling is self-care.

The journey through grief requires patience, compassion, and the willingness to embrace both the pain and the growth that comes with loss. Ultimately, finding our own path through grief involves self-reflection, self-care, and honouring our unique relationship.

Let Go of What-ifs

A milestone step in navigating our grief involves recognizing that we shouldn't diminish our genuine bond with our dog. That bond is real, and there's no benefit in convincing ourselves otherwise, or avoiding the depth of our feelings. We can honour the truth—that our dog's place in our lives was, and is, incredibly meaningful and significant.

If we weren't ready to let go or to say goodbye, our mind can question everything. We need to anchor ourselves to that connection instead of getting lost in "what if" scenarios. These thoughts will lead to endless possibilities, and ultimately force us to carry a heavier weight.

Guilt tricks us into believing we had more control or influence than we actually did, leading us further down a path of uncertainty and regret. Instead of dwelling on what we could have done differently, we must accept that some things are beyond our control. Dwelling on hypotheticals only brings more pain without any resolution.

Dogs cannot speak. Dogs are masters at hiding their pain. Sometimes, we must make the decision for our dog, and this can feel uncertain and unfair. We need to consider that dogs can't or won't tell us how they feel, what they want, or when they feel their quality of life has reached a point where they are ready for peace. We had no way of having this conversation—although I know I certainly tried!

So many doubts may wander through our mind. If we knew our dog was sick, should we have agreed to euthanasia earlier? Maybe we feel we should have agreed to a suggested surgery we didn't go forward with. Perhaps we did agree to surgery, and they died anyway. It's important to acknowledge that given the tools and information we had at the time, we did everything we could for that someone we loved.

Even if we could foresee that the treatment would work and they would be with us a little longer, but knew they would be in decline, would we have still decided to go ahead and try every option we could? Would we make a different decision and keep them here in pain? If we kept here while they were in pain, we can try and practice self-compassion that we made the best decision possible with our capacity at the time. And still, we tend to question our decision.

This is a normal reaction, but we must try to stop questioning ourselves. We had no way of knowing how things would end. We loved our dog and made the right choice for that moment in time. Besides, we can't place human limitations such as suggesting that our dog is upset with our decision, because dogs are the ultimate champions in the act of forgiveness.

Intrusive thoughts are normal, such as the moment of their death, or would've/could've/should've thoughts. The issue is there is no answer to fix it, and running through scenarios that never happened takes us out of living in the present, which is what we need to do to help our brain remap. Know that these types of thoughts will come, and that we do not have to entertain them.

The path to feeling reconnected and healthy is in front of us through learning to embrace and then release the pain. Exercising, crying, writing a letter, meditation, eating, sleeping, and therapy are all ways we can find release. If we don't eventually release what we no longer need, we get stuck or sick!

Our dog spent their life showing us how important we are in this world. They let us know that we deserve to feel loved. Now, we must allow our dog's love to continue in the form of a life lesson toward loving ourselves.

Just in case you need to hear this directly, you need to keep moving forward in this life because someone else needs your love now. That someone, is you. You are having a human experience, and whatever the circumstances, your dog forgives you and still loves you. Give yourself permission to feel your sadness; it is a form of self-care, and you also deserve to feel the gentle warmth of the sun. It's time to forgive yourself. Let it out, and let go of what-ifs. The following *Self-Care Moment* can be used as a guide.

Self-Care Moment: Letting Go of What-Ifs

This activity is designed to help you process and release the burden of "what-if" thinking and guilt, allowing you to focus on honouring your dog's memory with love and compassion.

Scan the QR code to complete this Self-Care Moment:

Death of a We

Your identity has shifted because your dog has died. It may feel like a piece of you is missing because your life is no longer defined in ways such as, "we are going for a walk" with your specific dog. You and your dog have been a *We* for years, so ask yourself, "What do I want?", and, "Who am I?" now that they are no longer alive.

Introducing a new activity in our life can help pair the experience so our brain knows there has been a shift. Dr. Mary Frances O'Connor is an associate professor of psychology at the University of Arizona, where she directs the grief and loss social stress lab. In an interview with O'Connor on the YouTube channel called Open to Hope, she explains she naturally started buying flowers when her cat died. When her cat was alive, her cat would have eaten the flowers and been sick, so she was able to enjoy fresh flowers in her home after the death of her cat. She notes that her brain started to use the cue of fresh flowers in her home to mean that her cat was not coming back.

Dr. O'Connor explains that we will never stop caring for our loved one. Instead, we are able to carry their love in their absence.

Improve Sleep & Manage Cortisol Rhythms

The grieving process is demanding not just emotionally but also cognitively and physically. It forces us to navigate and remap a deep emotional attachment that often spans years, while purging or creating distance from unhelpful memories.

Matthew Walker is a scientist and professor of neuroscience and psychology at the University of California. His book, *Why We Sleep: Unlocking the Power of Sleep and Dreams*, provides insight into the importance of sleep and mood, "The best bridge between despair and hope is a good night's sleep." During times of grief, getting good sleep can be challenging, but it is really important.

Sleep helps us stay emotionally balanced, and supports our brain's ability to reorganize itself. This amazing activity is called neuroplasticity.

As humans, our natural rhythm follows a diurnal pattern, meaning, we're wired to be active during the day and restful at night. While there are exceptions for night owls, our genetic and neural circuitry leans toward this diurnal cycle. When we do not get enough sleep, our mental and physical health starts to decline rapidly. Thankfully, Aura's wisdom shines through on how to navigate this!

Exposure to sunlight or sitting under a bright, full-spectrum artificial light in the morning can be a game-changer for improving sleep quality. This also assists with managing cortisol rhythms effectively, which in turn helps with our sleep cycle. Cortisol is often labelled as the stress hormone, but it plays many roles, including boosting our immunity, and helping our body to wake in the morning.

If we looked at our cortisol level throughout the day on a graph, having a flatter slope of cortisol throughout the day has been shown to correlate with complicated grief. This tells us that we want our cortisol to have a wave every day instead of being stagnant. We want to use the benefits of cortisol by encouraging it to be higher and lower at certain times of the day.

Serotonin is also affected by our exposure to light. This neurotransmitter is often associated with helping to lift depression. Light is thought to increase serotonin production and stop it from converting into melatonin, the hormone that makes us sleepy.

So, if we get early morning exposure to light, our body knows it is time to be awake and present, and it helps our body slip into the much-needed diurnal cycle so we can have a better night's sleep.

Sunlight can directly benefit our health in other ways, such as helping our body create vitamin D. Low levels of vitamin D have been linked to depression and anxiety. Higher levels are thought to help strengthen our immune system, which in turn can help prevent autoimmune diseases. Sun exposure also triggers the release of beta-endorphins, our natural painkillers that improve mood and reduce stress.

Finding a sunny spot next to a window while enjoying our morning cup of tea can help us get the benefits of better sleep and health. Sitting in nature in the morning sun is even more beneficial. Staying clear of bright artificial lights in the evening, such as our computers and phones also helps. This sets the stage for deep restorative sleep, which is pivotal for our emotional well-being—especially during grief.

Sleep isn't just about feeling refreshed. It's about facilitating neuroplasticity, our brain's rewiring process that occurs during deep sleep. Sleep is a main ingredient that can help us move through the grieving process. Basking in daylight and embracing a healthy sleep routine not only aids in emotional regulation and autonomic balance, but may also help our brain adapt to our new world.

Self-Care Moment: Sunlight Boost

A simple way to improve sleep and well-being is by getting sunlight early in the morning, even if it's not right at sunrise. This activity may have significant benefits for our overall health by helping to align our body's natural rhythms with the day-night cycle.

Scan the QR code to complete this Self-Care Moment:

Continue the Bond

We can find it really hard to accept that someone special is no longer here with us. Even though we can understand the facts logically, it's emotionally tough to come to terms with them. This is because our brains have pathways and connections that hold onto memories of what we lost, activating our attachment system, especially when we think about them or see things that remind us of them. It's like our brain is trying to act as if they're still here based on what we knew about them before, even though we know they're not here. This can be confusing and sometimes doesn't make sense, but it's how our brain works.

That said, using memories as a bridge is an essential step to continuing the bond within the grieving process. However we decide to do this is acceptable, as long as it doesn't cause harm or interfere with our functioning in daily life, or our relationships. Everyone is different in what works for them.

Know that it is also possible to be excessive with honouring our loved one. When enshrinement limits us our capacity to adapt, we may want to consider other ways to mourn. The other end of the spectrum is when we can only remember negative interactions regarding the loss. We must be honest with ourselves when reflecting on our experiences, and we may need support with the deeper work.

From an attachment perspective, children can learn to cope with being separated from their caregivers when they feel secure in their relationship with them. Similarly, we can find a new way to feel connected with our dog, and adjust to the physical separation caused by their death. It is true that they are no longer physically here, and we've been forced to adapt to a new reality.

I know this may feel hard to accept, but our connection with our dog continues even though they have crossed over the rainbow. Our attachment system is desperately trying to find a way to make sense of the circumstances, and feel reconnected in a different way. Research has studied the many ways we can explore reconnecting and continue the bond. The following are some examples:

Talking About Them

This might involve keeping memories active by talking about our dog. At first, I had a hard time remembering Aura in any other way than her final moments on earth. When this was all that came up in my initial therapy sessions after the death, my therapist was wise enough to say, "Tell me more about her, who she was, what did she love?" These simple questions opened my mind to remember the sad and the happy, which eventually led to me writing this book today.

Photos

Looking at or displaying photos of our dog helps us remember them and the love they brought into our lives, even though they're no longer with us physically. Photos help us to navigate that internal transition we have to make to accommodate the fact that they are no longer here. Photos are also a wonderful reminder of the role and love our dog provided us when they were alive, and continue to provide in our lives.

Take Their View

My next suggestion below plays off an idea a friend of mine, shared with me. He thinks it is important for us to pay attention to how dogs live fulfilling lives, and that we have a lot to learn from them.

Viewing the world through a dog's eyes makes life much simpler and more beautiful. Dogs seem to know how to invest in and live a good life. Life is full of positivity if we allow it to flow, and this can also help us make meaning of the experiences we had with our dog.

How to live life like a dog:
1. Always say hello and be curious about new friends.
2. Play until you are tired.
3. Choose kindness.
4. Try new things.
5. Smell the forest.
6. Set and respect boundaries.
7. Be kind to your body.
8. Make time for zoomies.
9. Get enough sleep.
10. Go for a walk—daily.
11. Know when to bark and when to bite.
12. Don't tell others you love them; show them!
13. Bask in the sunshine whenever possible.

Talk to Them

We can envision our loved one's perspective or use them as a role model. Going for walks in nature and imagining what they would say or feel about the walk if they were there can be grounding. We can also talk to them. Yes, I said it, we can talk to them in our minds or even out loud! Having conversations with the deceased can bring comfort and feelings of closeness, and can offer us guidance and support. Depending on the situation, this approach can also help us work through present-day decision-making.

Their Belongings

Keeping their belongings close, and holding onto them can provide comfort and a sense of connection. I still have all of Aura's items. My other dogs have adopted most of them, but one collar remains unused and is kept in a safe place. It's also understandable and very okay if your response was to get rid of all dog beds, bowls, collars, and leashes. It's not mandatory to keep them.

Honouring Them

Honouring the memory of our loved one is partially why we have funerals and, in some cultures, a set period of mourning and traditions. We can honour our dog with rituals, visiting special places, and including them in special events. For years after my grandfather passed away, my siblings and I would play cards after family dinner, just as we did with our grandpa. Setting a place at the table at a family dinner is okay, as long as it is understood that the place setting is for someone who is not going to walk through the door—the intention is to acknowledge they are physically gone forever.

We can do the same for our canine loved ones! We can still keep our dog's bowl on the floor, go for walks at the dog park, and have their leash hanging in the mudroom. When we continue traditions or visit places that are meaningful to us and our dog, it can help keep them present in our heart, and continue our connection to our community. Honouring our dog can look like a special Christmas ornament, wearing their collar as a bracelet, having photos or drawings of them on display, lighting a candle while thinking of them, placing their dog tag on a fence at a favourite dog park, or practicing to feel and expand pleasant sensations when recalling joyous memories. The list could go on.

Live with Purpose

We can actively live with purpose to make our loved one proud. This might look like changing our health or habits, or visiting that special place they never got to visit with us. Making positive changes in our lives to honour the memory of our loved one and knowing we're making them proud, can bring a sense of pride and fulfillment.

After-Death Communication

Finally, there is After-Death Communication (ADC)—we'll talk more about this in the last chapter of the book.

Acting out any of these suggestions is not a sign of prolonged grief disorder or complicated grief. They're just part of how we can experience the transformation of our connection.

Continuing the bond with our dog helps us acknowledge the new reality of our relationship with them. Communicating and connecting with them in various ways is not a mental health issue. I teach that it's important for health professionals and supportive individuals to understand this truth. It's beneficial to encourage the bereaved to maintain their bond with the deceased in a way that feels right for them.

The Story of Oscar: Gratitude Unleashed

Oscar was often seen as unlovable during his first years, due to his high energy and destructive behaviour. He was found in a garbage dumpster, and then bounced between homes, searching for the one that could accommodate his needs. Families who showed interest in him were quickly deterred by the exuberant nature and the chaos he seemed to bring wherever he went. His separation anxiety led to destructive tendencies, resulting in damage to property, and frustration among those who attempted to care for him.

Despite these challenges, Oscar's potential for love and companionship was evident to his owner, who could look beyond his behaviour. Instead of viewing him as a burden, she saw him as a diamond in the rough with immense love to give—if only given the chance.

Oscar's energy finally found purpose in adventures with his owner through hikes, lake trips, and snowshoeing. Commitment to meeting his needs and understanding his anxieties over the next seven years transformed Oscar into an obedient companion and a popular friend in the dog community. "We had a special connection, and I like to think he chose me to love him and carry on his memory."

Around age 13, Oscar woke up incontinent. By the time he was seen by the vet the next day he couldn't walk. He was given medicine, and they were told to go home and wait a few hours. If he was not better by then, they were to return. Oscar started to show signs of pain, and his owner knew this was going to mean goodbye.

In the next hour, Oscar's owner brought him to the park in a wagon and laid him on the grass. He was surrounded by love. His owner watched as each furry friends approached him, offering kisses, sniffs, and silent companionship, as if they knew it was a farewell gathering. Despite his deteriorating health,

Oscar seemed to find comfort in the presence of his companions.

His owner cradled Oscar as a series of seizures began. She was filled with sadness yet determined to ensure him a peaceful transition.

Oscar was welcomed back at the vet. "I promised him the best life, and I wasn't going to be selfish for my temporary well-being."

In his final moments, Oscar's owner stroked his fur and told him he was a good boy. She reminded him that he was loved and will always be loved. He opened his eyes, had a sip of water, and gave his owner a kiss. This was interpreted as a gentle gesture of goodbye, expressing his love and gratitude for the life they shared together. She held Oscar closer as he peacefully passed away, forever leaving behind one more cherished moment.

His body was taken home and buried in a special place in the country.

Even though Oscar's owner had more than a week off to grieve, she remembers struggling to concentrate at her busy job. It was then that she realized just how therapeutic Oscar's presence was. She was able to process her grief over the next two months while off work.

To further honour Oscar's memory and the deep bond they shared, his owner decided to get a tattoo of Oscar's paw print. It now serves as a permanent reminder of the love, loyalty, and joy that Oscar brought into her life. Oscar's legacy lives on in his owner's heart and through her tattoo.

Two years after Oscar's death, she adopted a new puppy named Junior. By sharing all of Oscar's favourite places to visit with Junior, she furthered her grieving journey.

Turn Within: How did your dog show you unconditional love?

Engage in Gratitude

There is a saying in neuroscience: Neurons that fire together, wire together.

The more we encourage our brain to practice a way of thinking or being, the more it wants to do it, and the easier it gets! I like to use the metaphor of a snowy toboggan hill with a bunch of kids sliding down the hill. As they slide down the hill they pack down a toboggan run, making it icier and faster. Think of the toboggan runs as neural networks.

Our brain works the same way. If we tend to have more depressing, helpless, controlling, or powerless thoughts, this might be because our thoughts and the environment encouraged those toboggan runs. Without meaning to, we've made those pathways super icy and easy to travel.

When we train our brain to focus on the positive aspects of our life, this leads to an increased sense of well-being and happiness. It is thought that the practice of expressing gratitude triggers the release of feel-good chemicals in the brain, such as dopamine and serotonin, and this can improve our mood and reduce our stress.

By regularly engaging in gratitude practices like the *Gratitude Rock* activity in the next *Self-Care Moment*, we're essentially rewiring our brain to become more attuned to the good things in our life, and to the present.

The more we focus on gratitude, the more our brain will naturally gravitate toward positive thoughts and experiences, and we will start to notice the value of life and everyone who contributes to it. By consistently focusing on gratitude, we're choosing to turn toward the sunny side of the hill!

Self-Care Moment: Gratitude Rock

Gratitude Rock is inspired by the idea that what you focus on grows new connections. My clients tell me that this exercise dramatically increases their capacity to be in the moment, and to find purpose and value in their lives. It is a helpful tool to increase your ability to tolerate feelings, and cultivate positivity in your life.

By deliberately choosing to focus on the things you are grateful for, you can train your brain to notice more of the good throughout your experiences. It also helps you to rewire your brain to be in the present moment.

This practice is requesting that you to start sliding down the sunny side of the toboggan hill with thick snow. I'm not going to lie; the first few times you try to slide down this side of the hill it's going to be annoying and difficult! The more you do it, the easier it will get.

Listen to the guided meditation here:

Just keep doing this all day, every day for at least a week, and you will likely notice a shift in how you feel in your world. An alternative to a rock is to use a coloured hair elastic around your phone. Even better if the hair elastic colour is the same as what you envisioned during the *Colour Breathing* meditation!

Notice as *Gratitude Rock* transforms your outlook on life, and enhances your overall sense of connection in the present.

Embracing New Realities

Accepting our dog's current state involves creating a new mental image of them, as this helps us place them in our three-dimensional map of space, time, and connection. Remapping how our dog exists in the present gives us as sense of closure. It encourages us to let go of fantasies or wishes that they are still with us physically, or that events had unfolded differently. Instead of dwelling on "what ifs", or trying to escape through substances or distractions, we can face reality and integrate their love into the present.

Writing a letter to our deceased loved one is considered expressive writing, which has been shown to have therapeutic benefits such as a sense of connection and meaning, and an overall improvement in emotional well-being. Reflecting on our dog through activities like writing can help us accept that they're no longer with us, and imagine where they might be now.

Seek Therapy & Community

While writing this book and dealing with the ongoing waves of grief-related clients, I needed to get composed. I knew the only way was to dive into literature and research grief. I also did my own therapy, and gained a sense of community by speaking with other specialists, and participating in professional training on the topic.

New loss can make past grief and trauma resurface, leaving us to deal with multiple losses and confusing feelings. When we're dealing with big feelings, it's important to have support, especially in the beginning of grief. Taking care of our bodies, surrounding ourselves with caring people, and talking about how we feel can make a big difference.

Sometimes, when we go through a really tough loss, our brains don't process the feelings and memories in a helpful way.

This can make us feel overwhelmed and extremely sad, making it hard to do regular things. It's like our minds get stuck on the sad parts, and we struggle to remember the good times. When this happens, we cannot access the more positive memories that we need to move through grief.

It's normal to feel upset or angry when we think about our pet being in pain or remember they are not with us anymore. These feelings usually lessen over time, and the intensity of the image fades, but sometimes they linger. When this happens, it's time to reach out for more professional support.

Eye Movement Desensitization and Reprocessing (EMDR)
EMDR is a well-researched therapy that was originally developed for trauma. Today, it is used for pretty much any mental health issue. It can also be helpful to expedite grief, even if we are not stuck. EMDR uses eye movements or tapping to invite the brain and body to have a thorough conversation, and to make connections. It helps us become unstuck, or expedites our processing of grief.

Whether or not we are stuck in our grief, therapy like EMDR can be helpful in moving us through grief faster. EMDR isn't a quick fix, but it can assist with a smoother grief journey.

The neat thing is that EMDR works with our brain and body in a natural way that we already do so to heal. EMDR helps us access our positive memories—the bridge—so we can feel them more strongly, and then properly file away the painful parts of our experience. This helps us to recall our memories in a less distressing and invasive way. It's like turning down the volume on the sad parts, which settles down the blizzard on the toboggan hill. Then, EMDR helps us access the sunny side of the hill, allowing us to remember our loved one with more connection and peace.

When we experience a traumatic loss, it can be appropriate to seek EMDR therapy within the first 24 hours. Doing so can reduce the risk of developing PTSD. If our loss was not traumatic, it is best to wait for grief counselling until we start to realize and really feel the sadness.

EMDR can also help us to finally resolve past trauma or loss that is blocking us from moving forward with our current grief. For example, if we experienced childhood trauma or had a difficult relationship with the deceased, we can find a more balanced perspective through EMDR. This might include realizing it's okay to feel sad, acknowledging how we've grown, or recognizing that the loss or the conflict in the relationship wasn't our fault.

After EMDR, clients often describe a feeling of literally having more distance from their upsetting memories, images, and thoughts. The memories don't change, but they don't feel as painful anymore, and they can suddenly focus on other parts of their story that were not so clear before.

EMDR therapy can set the stage for a sense of closure. The goal is for us to remember our deceased loved one beyond our painful memories. As we enjoy reexperiencing our positive memories, we remap where our loved one is in space, time, and attachment. This invites the possibility of bringing them to mind while at the same time experiencing a sense of peace.

This is helpful because if the disturbing memories no longer feel intrusive or overwhelming, there is no need to continue using coping skills to keep the upset at bay. It means we don't have to work as hard to push away sad thoughts, and with more energy to grow and evolve, we can adapt to our new world. While EMDR won't change the fact that someone is gone, it can remove emotional barriers that prevent us from forming new connections and relationships.

The following was unsolicited feedback from a client after they were discharged from my care. They had experienced EMDR to help with the loss of their dog, and gave me permission to quote them.

The EMDR clearly worked: I ran into someone yesterday who I hadn't seen in years and who was unaware of Oskar's passing and, for the first time, was able to relay the news without an emotional meltdown. So, thank you!

EMDR isn't for everyone or for every stage of grief. It works best when we're ready to face our feelings and stay present in the therapy session. For EMDR to be effective, we need to be able to access the painful feelings while at the same time, be grounded in the present.

If feeling the deep pain is too hard right now, that's okay. Self-care and other supportive therapy can still be helpful as we take care of ourself.

Cognitive Behavioural Therapy (CBT)
CBT can help us focus on understanding and changing our negative thoughts and behaviours related to our grief. For example, if we constantly blame ourselves for the loss, CBT can help us challenge these thoughts and find more realistic perspectives. CBT has been found to be helpful in teaching coping strategies to deal with tough emotions that come with grief. With CBT, we can learn practical ways to handle our feelings throughout our daily lives.

Both EMDR and CBT have been studied extensively, and both can be effective. They have different approaches, though. CBT helps us change how we think and behave. On the other hand, EMDR focuses more on processing past, present, and future experiences to integrate the positive and adaptive information that already lies within us.

Researchers have compared EMDR and CBT as a therapeutic intervention for grief. Both therapies have improved well-being, reduced symptoms, and helped people cope better. Those who tried CBT felt confident with tools to manage their emotions going forward, while those who tried EMDR, felt more distance from upsetting memories. It's like CBT helps us cope with the surface stuff, and EMDR helps us heal deep down so the feelings aren't overwhelming in the first place.

Narrative Therapy

This is another therapy approach often used for grief. Here, we explore and reshape the stories we tell ourselves about our loss, and how it has affected us. By changing these stories to fact and understanding where they came from, we can understand our grief better and find new ways to cope and grow.

For example, narrative therapy can help us rewrite the story in our mind that we will never be happy again, to a more helpful narrative that acknowledges our pain, but also leaves room for hope and healing.

Mindfulness-based Therapies

This includes many approaches, such as meditation. These methods help us focus on being present in the moment and accepting our thoughts and feelings without judgment. By practicing mindfulness, we become more resilient in managing our emotions. Mindfulness techniques can help us ground ourselves in the present moment and find calmness and clarity when we are feeling overwhelmed. This assists us with feeling our way through the pain of grief.

Mindfulness is often used alongside other helpful approaches, such as yoga, EMDR and CBT.

Group Therapy or Grief Communities

Feeling that we are part of a community can be incredibly healing on our journey. When we share our story surrounded by others who've experienced loss, we realize that although our grief is unique, we're not alone. We tend to find comfort in knowing that others understand what we're going through, and we can also evolve through their experiences.

Self-Care Moment: Practicing Being Present

As you navigate through your grief, it's important to be present and connected to your emotions and surroundings. You can acknowledge and embrace your feelings of loss without getting lost in memories or wishing for a different reality. Let's ground in the present moment to prepare for staying grounded when big waves of emotion come. You can write about your experience afterward to reflect.

Listen to the guided meditation here:

CHAPTER SIX: *ACROSS THE BRIDGE*

Aura's Pizza Party Hello

Lemon's warm fur under the blanket comforted me as I woke up. Heart racing, I tried to banish the unsettling images that lingered from my dream. I struggled to shake off the sadness that had seeped into my waking world. The void of Aura's absence was once again emanating from my chest.

This recent dream took place in a beautiful beach town I'd never visited before. The weather was sunny and warm, and I found myself alone in this picturesque setting. It started with me riding a scooter searching for a meal. That's when I spotted a charming wooden food hut by the ocean, drawing me in with its inviting appearance. As I stepped inside, the radio softly played music from the 1930s, creating a nostalgic atmosphere.

To my surprise, the hut was deserted. I called out, "Hello?" but received no response. Curious, I peered over the counter and discovered a messy scene, as if a food fight had just taken place, with pepperoni, cheese, and fresh peppers scattered everywhere.

As I looked around, I noticed Aura, my Heart Dog, lying there peacefully in the sunshine. She gazed up at me serenely. Just as I was about to rescue her from this place, the dream abruptly came to an end.

Although the dream itself should not have been disturbing, my emotions of being with Aura so vividly jolted me back into my grief. By evening, my mood had not improved, and when someone brought up the topic of loss at the dinner table, I thought it would be helpful to share my experience with my family.

"I had a dream last night of Aura. I don't know why it is so upsetting for me."

One of the younger kids said, "It's okay Mom, I still miss Aura too."

"Thanks, buddy," Tears rose to the surface, but I held them back, "I guess what I don't understand is why she was alone in a food hut, surrounded by pizza toppings everywhere—she was just laying there in the sun, like as if she had just finished eating these scraps to the point where her only choice was to sleep in the sun!"

My mind darted to unthinkable scenarios: *Did she feel abandoned? Was there a fight? Did she want me to rescue her? It was just a dream. Just a dream!*

There was a pause in the conversation, and then one of the older teens smiled and said, "Well, I don't know about you, but to me, that sounds like heaven for Aura. Cheese, peppers, and pepperoni? She would love that!"

It's true. She loved cheese, peppers, pepperoni—and sunshine. The void in my chest filled up once again with a golden warmth. The realization that Aura was saying hello, not goodbye, was exactly what I needed.

A Book Haunting

I'm sharing my personal experience because it is important to normalize and embrace events we cannot explain. I always knew I wanted to write a book, and when it came time for me to take this task more seriously, I could not decide on a topic. I'm not religious, but I believe that if you ask the Universe questions, it answers. Sometimes, the answer comes as an idea popping into my mind, a clue within a conversation with someone, or through coincidental events. As I learned in my experience, the answers can be blunt harsh truths, and we should be thoughtful about what we ask for.

So, I decided to ask for guidance: *Universe, I'm unsure what to write about, so please send me a sign.* That very day, I had my first client grappling with profound grief. It caught me off guard and pushed me out of my comfort zone. As a trauma therapist, I was accustomed to helping individuals navigate childhood traumas, car accidents, or traumatic adult experiences. However, this client's recent return from a vacation brought news of their beloved dog's passing. The weight of their grief was palpable, and I could sense the heaviness in their energy as they shared their sorrow. It struck a chord within me, triggering emotions I hadn't anticipated. I wasn't prepared for my own grief to be activated. After the session, I found myself overwhelmed with tears, mourning not only for their loss, but also for the reminder of the void left behind by Aura's absence.

That's odd, I mused to myself. It had been some time since I last thought about Aura, and I believed I had moved past the depths of my grief. Moreover, I rarely struggled with containing my emotions. Taking a deep breath, I prepared for the next client session.

This time, my client delved into their strained relationship with their child, a familiar topic. However, the unexpected twist was that their child was grappling with the recent loss of their grandparent's dog, who had passed away six months ago. The family had taken on the responsibility of caring for the dog after the grandparents' passing, only for it to pass away shortly thereafter in their care.

As my client spoke, I could feel a surge of grief welling up inside me, threatening to spill over like an overflowing sewer system. *This isn't acceptable,* I scolded myself, grasping at composure.

Then I wondered if this was the book idea I was supposed to go with. On my way home, I looked up at the sky and whispered, *Aright, Universe, let's try again tomorrow. Please send me a message of what I need to write a book about.*

The next day, I had a client mention it was their deceased dog's birthday, and so they were feeling sad. This atypical theme continued throughout the week, with nearly every client sharing stories of loss related to their dogs and emphasizing the vital role these pets played in their mental and physical well-being. This sudden focus on dog-related grief during sessions felt unfamiliar and unsettling for me, and I did not like it at all!

Nope, not doing this! I firmly told myself, *I do not want to revisit my pain of Aura, and just to prove this is not what I'm supposed to write about Universe, I challenge you. Have my child client mention the grief of a dog this Friday.* I felt clever, knowing that this client's family didn't have a dog, so the odds seemed in my favour.

That Friday, my young client bounced into the therapy room with his usual energy. As we began to build a rocket ship with magnetic blocks, he suddenly shared, "I'm feeling really sad because I miss my cat who died in the summer."

Aha! I thought to myself, *not a dog!*

We moved into talking through the loss of his beloved pet cat. We used some EMDR-related techniques, which seemed to reduce his upset about his loss. As the session drew to a close, I felt relieved that I wasn't fated to write a book centered on the grief and loss of dogs.

My hand was on the doorknob, I remembered to ask, "Oh, I almost forgot, how was your Christmas?"

He replied, "Christmas was great! Grammy and Grampy visited, and we had a lot of fun—except they were feeling sad because their dog died on Christmas day." Goosebumps prickled across my skin, and my knees nearly buckled under me. I was in shock.

I walked him to the waiting room, and on my way back to my office I felt a rush of anger through me. *Nope! Not good enough!* I thought to myself, *Universe, if you want me to write a book on the grief and loss of a dog, then you better send me a sign that is so obvious when I get home that I cannot deny it! And, please, do not hurt my current dogs.* I chuckled to myself; there was absolutely nothing I could think of that would knock my socks off as per my demand.

When I got home, I found my husband working at his desk in our bedroom as usual. I gave him a kiss, and the bed caught my eye. On it, was a photo of Aura that was taken a few weeks before she passed away. Seeing that picture made me realize the Universe had won. My eyes filled with tears as I hugged her photo close to me.

"What is this doing here?" I blurted.

My husband immediately tuned into my response. "So sorry, Hun, I should have put that away." He went on to inform me that earlier that morning, our son was getting ready for school, rolling on the bed, and missing Aura while looking at the photo. "I didn't think you'd be home so soon, and I didn't get around to putting it away." He reached for the photo.

"No, it's okay," I sobbed. "It was meant to be here for me to see."

I conceded to the idea that this was my mission; I would learn about grief, confront my grief, and write a book about grief—of a dog. I became immersed in the professional development side of my research, and I was surprised to learn that I was already working with grief as a trauma therapist. I realized that within all trauma lies grief, but not all grief is traumatic. Not only was I already qualified on the topic, but I also accepted that this project was needed as part of my healing journey.

As time went by, I wrote whenever I had the chance. But as I worked on the book, doubts crept in. I started to wonder if this was really what I should be focusing on. COVID-19 interrupted our world, placing high demand on my services as a therapist, while at the same time balancing five kids in the house and dealing an additional legal issue with my ex-husband. I was starting to feel burnt out, and the last thing I wanted to do was think about the loss of my best friend.

I decided to go on a work-related training and wellness retreat. I thought it would be a good opportunity to recharge. I also invited my mother along so she could enjoy the beautiful location while I attended the sessions. One night, I told her about the book. The only other people who knew about my book were a few select others. I shared how I felt torn, especially after sitting next to someone who loved seeing photos of my current dogs on my phone that day. It made me realize that I needed to find closure about Aura. I wasn't sure if I should keep going with writing the book or not.

The following day, I was seated in my usual spot, waiting for the training to start, when I felt a gentle tap on my shoulder. I turned around to a warm smile. "Krista, I hope this is okay to mention, but I overheard you talking about your dogs yesterday," she began. "I woke up this morning with this strong feeling that I should show you something. My husband Tom recently retired and discovered he's quite talented at drawing. He's found his niche in creating portraits of dogs who have passed away as a special keepsake for their owners. I know your dogs are alive, but I just had this strong sense that I needed to share his work with you. Would you like to see some photos of his drawings?"

And with that, she proceeded to show me a collection of beautifully detailed pencil drawings, each honouring the essence of the dogs in a remarkably lifelike manner.

"Wow, his work is amazing!" my eyes swelling with tears, knowing the Universe was sending yet another nudge to me about my book, "I need to share a story with you about a book I almost wasn't going to write…"

From that moment, I have been fully committed to writing this book. I fear it will literally haunt me if I don't!

Although I've decided to continue writing the book, the connection and messages with Aura have not stopped. For example, I was on an airplane across the country, and suddenly, I felt Aura's presence next to me. It was a surreal experience because she had passed away two years prior, yet I could sense her presence so vividly—while on an airplane of all places! I really felt as if she was around me, right there. There was no reason for me to think of her at that moment; the sensation just happened spontaneously. I smiled and allowed myself to bask in her comforting warmth.

The following day, while shopping with my daughters, I stumbled upon a trinket that caught my eye—an intricately designed rock adorned with metal coins shaped like a paw and a heart. Not only did it not fit in with all the other crafts, but the decorations immediately reminded me of a stone I recently lost that was a reminder of Aura. Suddenly, I felt a rush of her love in my chest. I wondered if Aura was once again trying to say hello, and I felt comfort in the thought that she was okay.

Were these experiences merely coincidences? Was the influx of grief-related clients' only chance occurrences and the encounter with the pencil portraits simply an opportunity to connect and start a friendship? Was the airplane experience just the altitude, and the rock just a cheesy trinket? Was my dream about Aura and the pizza toppings just a dream that I'm overly reading into it? Or perhaps, more likely, these are examples of my After-Death Communication experiences. Although the idea of communicating with the deceased can sound scary, these experiences are well-documented and researched in science. These ongoing connections have helped me navigate and find meaning in my new world.

Energy Cannot Be Created or Destroyed

Many people share experiences of After-Death Communication in various ways. This can involve seeing, hearing, feeling, or even smelling the presence of the deceased. I hope that in the future, we'll gain a deeper understanding of these experiences and what they mean regarding what happens after death. Such insights could be a valuable guide for humanity.

Albert Einstein once said, "Energy cannot be created or destroyed; it can only be changed from one form to another." While adding this statement in this book isn't intended as a physics lesson, it does highlight the interconnectedness between physical and metaphysical realms. We still have so much to learn about consciousness and quantum physics.

If you're interested in delving into the fascinating research in this area, there are numerous studies that offer valuable insights. Some of these I've referenced in writing this book. Their scientific approach helps us evolve our understanding of life, death, and the potential for continued connection beyond the physical realm.

What Should We Believe?

Each of us holds beliefs that brings comfort when facing death, and it's valuable to remain open to different perspectives while we honestly reflect on our experiences.

While we can connect with the sense of love by remembering and imagining our loved ones, the question arises: can they also connect with us? It's worth noting that our understanding of the world has evolved significantly over time. Just as we once believed the earth was flat and diseases were caused by demons, scientific discoveries continue to challenge and expand our knowledge about life and death. Have you ever entered a room and sensed tension without knowing the situation? Some might say this is the same as reading someone else's energy. This concept could possibly be supported by the understanding of mirror neurons, which help us to sense and share emotions with others. Quantum physics, too, presents fascinating possibilities with its ongoing discoveries.

You might have heard stories of people experiencing communication with the deceased during near-death moments or on their deathbeds. As a former social worker in a hospital, I observed that such bedside visions often signaled that a person's time was drawing near, prompting us to notify their loved ones to come to the hospital for a final goodbye.

Throughout history, people have shared perceptions of connecting with the deceased, often viewing it as a profound experience of growth and connection. Many believe that the soul or energy of the deceased exists beyond their physical body and the earthly realm. The idea that we have a body and soul that separate After-Death, and join a grand space has been a constant thread throughout our human existence, and has persisted across cultures and religions. I feel that connections and contact with the deceased have shaped our beliefs and who we are as a species.

While science hints at the existence of a bond between the living and the dead, our full understanding remains incomplete. What the research does say, is that whether or not these experiences are real is irrelevant. What matters is that they happen—all the time—and experiencers seem to benefit from this. This is especially true with a Heart Dog.

The Story of Zieli: Warmth

Described as a soul dog, Zieli was a Jack Russell silky mix, whose intelligence and unique personality made her an adored presence in the household. Zieli had a routine of greeting her owner with her favourite toy every time she returned home. She loved her treats, food, and her Mario toy. Zieli was not the biggest fan of new people or other dogs, but was very loyal to her family.

Zieli's life was not without challenges; she battled a painful and stubborn skin condition involving hair follicle cysts. This required regular care, medications for pain relief, and multiple surgeries.

Shortly after the death of her owner's father, Zieli's started to have mobility issues in her back legs. This was all very upsetting for Zieli's owner.

Despite seeking help from a dog physio and the vet, Zieli's condition seemed to improve temporarily before worsening again with distressing breathing issues. This prompted Zieli's owner to make the difficult decision to let her go.

Surrounded by family members at home, Zieli was offered her favourite treats as a final gesture of love. Upon arriving at the vet, Zieli's owner recalls not being able to get out of the car for some time. "I imagined being able to go away with her where she would be better. It was so hard to do."

Zieli's final moments were peaceful, and her owner was relieved that she had a good death.

The loss of Zieli left a profound impact on her owner. She sometimes feels she let her dog live for longer than she should have, because she couldn't imagine a life without her. "It was a relief when it did happen, that she was no longer in pain, and I was lucky to have had fifteen years with her."

With three other elderly dogs at home needing attention and love, Zieli's owner was reminded of the importance of caring for those still with her.

She believes she provided Zieli with the best care possible, which brings a sense of peace amidst her grief. "I am surprised about how resilient I have been."

Zieli is now imagined as being reunited with her owner's father—a fellow animal lover—in a peaceful and joyful place beyond this world. Her owner envisions Zieli enjoying this existence while no longer in pain, and uses this imagery as one of her safe places if she can't sleep or is missing other pets. When she does this, she feels a warmth in her chest and finds this helps to prepare for another impending wave of grief.

When reflecting on the emotional pain that comes with loving a dog, Zieli's owner wants others to know that the only time our dog breaks our hearts is when they have to say goodbye. If they could, they would stay with us forever.

Turn Within: How did your dog make you feel special?

Self-Care Moment: Hello Again

Visualizing talking to our loved one can be a very powerful technique. In this activity, you will have an opportunity to imagine having an interaction with them in the present. The key here is to speak to them, not about them.

Although tempting, please skip this exercise for now if you are early in your grieving process where you're feeling numb, or needing additional support for your grief or your mental health.

Listen to the guided meditation here:

Our Connection Never Dies

Have you ever sensed the presence of someone who has died? Have you heard their voice calling your name, or did they somehow offer you guidance? Perhaps you suddenly noticed a smell that reminded you of them. Maybe you saw them as if they were still alive or felt a hug as if they were physically there with you. Did they visit you in an extremely clear and coherent dream? These are examples of scientifically documented After-Death Communication (ADC).

ADC is any experience perceived as a sensed or direct contact with the deceased. This is a normal and healthy human experience. ADC does not happen for everyone, but it can happen at any age, and with every culture, gender, ethnicity, education level, or religious belief. Even those who do not believe in an afterlife can experience one!

Most people find these experiences healing and transformative, and almost always, the experiencer receives some sort of comforting message from the deceased. Research shows that it doesn't actually matter if ADC is real; what matters is that experiencers benefit from them. You may have experienced an ADC and not realized it, or perhaps you did, and now you have a name for it.

This was certainly the case for me. I now realize I've witnessed many ADC experiences amidst processing grief with EMDR with my clients, and have heard many client's stories.

ADC experiences are quite common and normal. Although we cannot explain why these events happen, we can prove that they actually do happen—a lot. In fact, studies indicate that a significant portion of the population has had an ADC at some point in their lives. It turns out that about 40% to 50% of people have experienced an ADC! And this is just the people who were asked and were brave enough to admit it.

Studies show that an ADC can be comforting and supportive for people dealing with their loss. These experiences can provide us with a sense of continuity and growth, helping us feel cared for, loved, and understood. They may also help us resolve conflicts we had in the relationship with the deceased, and boost our confidence in problem-solving and decision-making in our new world reality.

An ADC can happen in various ways and under different circumstances. These experiences aren't limited to a specific state of consciousness; they can occur while awake, during sleep, meditation, or as part of a near-death experience. They can also happen to anyone, regardless of their health condition, ranging from perfectly healthy individuals to those nearing the end of life. ADC can happen with deceased loved ones, and with the deceased we don't know, such as someone who died in a car accident that we were involved with.

After-Death Communication can manifest in various ways:
Visual
This means seeing the deceased, either as if they're physically there or in your mind's eye.

Auditory
It means hearing sounds or voices associated with the deceased or hearing their voice.

Tactile
This is about feeling touches or sensing the physical presence of the deceased, such as feeling them sit on the bed, or touch your hand.

Olfactory
This refers to smelling scents connected to the deceased, even if you can't find where the smell is coming from.

Sentient
This is when you sense the presence of the deceased without any specific senses being involved. For example, you might feel like

they're nearby, or they visit you in a dream that's clearer and more memorable than usual.

Different types of ADC experiences:
Spontaneous
An After-Death Communication (ADC) often occurs unexpectedly, without deliberate effort to make it happen. Many of my clients have shared their personal experiences with me, and I have witnessed such occurrences firsthand during therapy sessions.

One compelling insight from my research for this book is that ADC seems to occur more frequently when individuals are in a deep state of openness and calm. This finding, combined with my training and clinical work, inspired me to develop a specialized framework for grief therapy called EMDR-GRIEF.

I now train EMDR clinicians in this innovative approach and offer it to the community as a meaningful tool for navigating grief and fostering healing.

Facilitated
Facilitated ADC experiences are often self-induced through specific practices, such as the use of a dark room and mirror in a process known as psychomanteum.

Because ADC can evoke profound emotions, involving a trained mental health professional is highly recommended. Professional support ensures you have the tools and guidance needed to navigate these experiences in a way that promotes overall wellness and emotional balance.

Assisted
Although there is more peer-reviewed research regarding spontaneous and facilitated ADC, research indicates they can also occur as assisted with a medium, or using tools such as psychedelics, cards, or specialized technology called Instrumental Transcommunication (ITC).

Requested
These are intentionally initiated by the person seeking the experience. This would include setting an intention during meditation.

As mentioned, ADC experiencers often receive comforting messages from the deceased. These messages can come in various forms, such as hearing the deceased's voice, sensing a knowing, or receiving a gesture or meaningful symbol. Most often, these messages are received telepathically. The messages from the deceased are usually reassuring. They may tell us not to worry about them, assure us that they are okay now without pain or troubles, and encourage us to live life fully without letting grief hinder us.

Sometimes, the messages address resolving conflicts from when they were alive. The deceased in the ADC may offer apologies or forgiveness, helping to settle old disputes and bringing closure to unresolved issues.

Most of us who've had an ADC report these events as reaffirming, noticing a grander continued connection. An ADC can give us hope that we will one day be reunited with our loved one, and help us feel reassured of the ongoing loving bond.

Not all ADCs are perceived as positive right away. For some, the experience can be intrusive and upsetting. This is especially true if it is from a member of the deceased with whom we had an unresolved conflict. Fortunately, finding a mental health professional who is understanding and experienced in this area can help us to work through this.

So, if there is all this research, and we know that ADCs are real, why don't we really know what it is like over the rainbow? Unfortunately, studies show that most messages from the deceased do not describe their circumstances in detail. Instead, messages focus on the deceased's state, such as that they are happy and alive in their new state and place, and they want us to carry on living life fully here.

Talking about ADC experiences can be challenging. Many hesitate to share due to fear of judgment from others. Terms like paranormal, mysterious, alleged, imaginal, or supernatural are sometimes used in dismissive or fantastical ways, which can be unhelpful.

Culture and personal beliefs also play a role in how an ADC is perceived and managed. Some traditions may look down on speaking ill of the dead, therefore restricting one from seeking emotional support.

It's crucial for healthcare providers and our support network to acknowledge and validate ADC experiences. Unfortunately, ADC can carry a lot of stigma, even within circles like the medical and helping professions. This stigma often stems from outdated training that ongoing contact with the deceased is unhealthy for grieving individuals.

ADC events and continuing the bond behaviours are not automatic signs of mental illness, and shouldn't be dismissed or judged negatively. Instead, potential significance and meaning should be explored with sensitivity and openness.

Ultimately, what matters most is that we find comfort and benefit from our ADC, regardless of whether others perceive them as "real" or not. Receiving support and understanding can make a meaningful difference in our healing journey, but at the end of the day, we know what we experienced!

During the writing of this book, I found myself contemplating how my personal views and experiences would be perceived. Although I feel confident in the state of my mental health and my personal experiences, I wonder how I will be judged for sharing my views and experiences in this area. This should not be the case, but unfortunately this is reality. For that reason, I've chosen carefully what to share in public.

If you've had an ADC, I hope this book helps you feel that your experience is normal and encourages open discussions about these meaningful encounters. The bond you have with your dog is special and forever. Whatever your own experience or belief might be, it's valid as long as it doesn't cause harm to you or others. If it helps you navigate your grief and hold onto a sense of connection rather than despair, embrace it fully!

Even if you haven't had an ADC experience, your bond with your dog will evolve into a form that suits your healing journey. Your relationship with them will naturally transform, allowing you to adjust and find meaning in your relationship.

Making Meaning of an ADC

While hallucinations can be defined as one's unique perceptions that others can't perceive, After-Death Communication (ADC)—also known as bereavement hallucinations—can appear similar. The difference is that with an ADC, the bereaved see, feel, or hear someone they've recently lost, whereas psychosis hallucinations typically consist of random content that may play into a theme which is detached from reality. Also, with psychosis, the person is not able to discern what is real. Those who've had an ADC are aware of how the experience is perceived by others. Also, unlike typical hallucinations related to psychosis, people experiencing an ADC often feel a loved one's presence without it involving any of the five senses. Finally, an ADC can be shared among more than one person at the same time.

The high rate of reported ADC experiences in people who are not diagnosed with psychosis, suggests that a healthy continuing bond exists between the living and the dead. Whether or not these experiences are true connections to the deceased is an important belief, however, it is the meaning we make of these experiences that truly matters.

An ADC brings comfort, a sense that the relationship continues, and that we will also continue. Often, an ADC brings a sense of personal growth, and can provide us with reassurance and encouragement to help us to accommodate and assimilate our grief. These experiences leave us feeling cared about and loved. They help us to forgive, and help feel forgiven. They can eliminate ongoing internal conflict. These experiences expedite our grief.

If we experienced an ADC and it felt comforting or positive, we can embrace the experience as a source of connection with the other side. However, if the ADC felt scary or intrusive, it's important to acknowledge our feelings, and seek support. It's understandable that encountering the unexpected presence of the deceased might feel overwhelming or unsettling. Even when inviting one, many people experience a mix of emotions when confronted with an ADC, including fear, confusion, or even disbelief. These reactions are entirely normal and valid, and they don't diminish the significance of our experience.

My message is, an ADC is healthy and can be a catalyst of change. We should allow ourselves space and time to navigate how they impact us, and reach out for support when we need it.

Many people yearn for a sign or message from their departed loved one as a way to find comfort, closure, or reassurance. As not everyone experiences an ADC, it's essential to remember that not having one does not diminish the significance of your relationship, or the impact they had on our life. We can honour our feelings and desires while remaining open to the possibility of finding other sources of comfort and connection in our grief journey.

Above all, we must trust in the enduring bond that we share with our dog. I believe that love transcends physical boundaries and continues to connect us even in their absence.

The Story of Nelson: Childhood Healing & ADC

Nelson's owner was eight years old when he was adopted. His owner had recently lost her older sister to meningitis, and her mother was struggling as a single mom. He was a welcomed temple of joy for his family, seen as a gift from the other side.

The bond between Nelson and his owner was profound, marked by shared moments of laughter, understanding, and mutual companionship. Through the years, Nelson's supportive role continued, especially during the owner's adolescence and early adulthood. His presence became synonymous with a sense of understanding, offering a lifeline through heartbreaks, first loves, and other life challenges.

Nelson passed away at sixteen years old due to cancer. His death reignited the emotional childhood loss of his owner's sister.

In the months following Nelson's crossing over the rainbow, his owner experienced intuitive feelings that they attribute to Nelson's continued presence in their life. "I know that spirits and energy never die. That energy is transmuted into another form."

One significant After-Death Communication (ADC) experience occurred through a healing dream, where Nelson and his owner were reunited at the beach, symbolizing a joyful reunion and a reminder of the deep bond they shared. In this dream, they swam together, reliving cherished memories. As they basked in the love that transcends earthly boundaries, Nelson's presence in the dream provided comfort and reassurance.

Beyond dreams, his owner and her husband also state they've experienced subtle yet profound signs of Nelson's presence. Feeling his energy and warmth, they have sensed him jumping up onto their bed and lying on their feet, a familiar gesture from their time together. These moments have brought a sense of peace and comfort, reinforcing the belief that Nelson's spirit continues to watch over them and their family.

Nelson's owner believes in broad spiritual connections with departed loved ones. She finds comfort in the idea of one day reuniting with Nelson, alongside her mother, sibling, and other beloved pets in the afterlife.

Turn Within: Have you had or heard of someone else having an ADC?

Self-Care Moment: ADC Reflection Worksheet

This activity invites you to look deeper into your After-Death Communication, if you've had one. Follow the instructions below to document your journey, and seek support as needed.

Scan the QR code to complete this Self-Care Moment:

CHAPTER SEVEN: *FINAL THOUGHTS*

Bailey: A Soft Goodbye

Shortly after I reviewed my first draft for this book, my siblings and our children were all invited over to my parent's home to say a final goodbye to my parents' dog Bailey. Claire Place Veterinary Hospice was scheduled to arrive the next day.

We awkwardly sat in a circle on chairs in the living room, the children not sure what to expect. As Bailey wandered from chair to chair to get a treat with each stop, her determined legs wobbled. My Dad had his best face on, and both of my parents were calmly engaging with their grandchildren. Saying goodbye is never easy, no matter how old you are, and my parents modelled the message that although this was sad, it was going to be okay.

Ironically, the box of cookies on the table had the label *Celebration* on it. As the group acknowledged this, there was an uncomfortable silence in the room. "Hey kids," I said, "make sure you don't give Bailey any of these chocolate cookies because..." In unison, everyone looked at me and then laughed out loud. Understandably, that might not be the most appropriate joke for everyone, but I had read the room well, and it broke the tension.

When it was time to leave, the children gave Bailey a final goodbye snuggle, and we went home so my parents could have some quiet time during their last night with her.

I cannot express enough how much of an honour it was to be asked to join Bailey for her final moments on earth. As I arrived at my parents' place the next day, an unfamiliar feeling swept over me. For the first time, I was there to support them, not the other way around. My Dad and I had bonded over loving our dogs, and I'm so thankful that dogs helped us with that connection. My parents welcomed me with a hug, and I gave Bailey a quick snuggle.

About half an hour later, the doorbell rang, and it was the same vet who had assisted us with Aura. Just as before, the vet's gentle presence set the stage for a calm and dignified crossing. Bailey was already resting on my father's lap as per usual, as content as can be, with her body drooping and molded over his legs. He opted to hold her as is for the rest of the time.

After the first injection of medicine to help her relax, Bailey fell asleep and started to snore loudly. Her cute pink tongue was poking out.

As we waited for my dad to be ready to give Bailey the final medication, my parents conversed about how wonderful it was that she could die in her home, where she felt safe and loved, as she was always so afraid at the clinic. Her lived experience from being a dog in the dumpster to having her final moments feeling safe and loved was acknowledged.

The vet was given the go ahead to continue with the procedure. Bailey's breath slowed peacefully, then stopped. My parent's quiet tears followed. I walked over to her lifeless body and lovingly cupped her face. I thanked her for loving my dad as deeply as she did, and imagined her being greeted by Aura and Banana over the rainbow.

A few days after Bailey died, I called my dad to see how he was doing. His voice became emotional over the phone when he said, "We thought we heard her last night, then we realized she wasn't there." As they were settling into bed, they both thought they heard her familiar low "huff", asking to go outside. My dad also described hearing her nails clicking on the floor at night, a common report I've heard shortly after a dog has passed. When I asked him if this was upsetting, he said no, that it was comforting. Thank you, Bailey, for saying hello.

Turn Within: What do you need right now for self-care? Take a moment now.

Kit: A Wave of Grief

My parents had all of Bailey's things packed in bags for me to donate. When I got home, I opened the bag and pulled out small ceramic food and water bowls. They belonged to Kit, my cat who passed away about 16 years ago. Kit was my first child, and she was there to welcome my human children into this world.

I had completely forgotten that I gave my parents her bowls when they adopted Bailey. Kit and I had a complicated relationship—I loved her to the moon and back, and she enjoyed attacking my ankles at 2 a.m. Kit had no issue expressing her disapproval of our selfish need to leave the house for work. When my ex-husband and I would return after a long day, it was not uncommon to enter a home with potting soil streaked over the front of the kitchen cupboards. She loved the water, and would often join us at the edge of the shower or play with a drip of water from the bathroom tap. She also loved Christmas trees, to the point that we couldn't have one anymore.

Grief invites grief, no matter how long ago the loss. I stood there holding her bowls and felt a wave of emotions overcome me. I teared up as I placed her bowls in my cupboard as a memento. Then I smiled and felt a warmth in my chest as I remembered how she initiated me into parenthood, how I worried about her when she had emergency surgery and lost her leg, and how much joy she'd bring when she attacked me from unimaginable places—like the top of a Christmas tree.

And so, I now also envision Kit in the scenery, over the rainbow. I see her high up on the rocks, overlooking her canine buddies and playing in the waterfall. Bailey is sitting pain-free by the calm water below, as her puppy-like eyes dart back and forth at playful fish. Banana is chewing her ball in the shade, and Aura is sleeping in the sun on the warm rocks. All of them are in their best states of health, feeling content as they wait for their next hello.

Turn Within: How would you like to envision your pet in their best state—over the rainbow?

A Letter to Grief

Dear Grief,

May I call you The Void? Your words captured the pain of my loss, and the heaviness of your presence. You are still like a shadow that never leaves, reminding me of my ongoing love and mild aching for Aura.

Reluctantly, I've begun to accept the depth of how you've helped me. I've learned that you are not just a visitor; you are a constant companion, teaching me life lessons that are both difficult and profound. This journey I'm on is certainly full of ups and downs! I've had moments that make me cry and memories that make me smile, but through it all, there has been your promise that I'd find meaning and purpose. I've grown and changed over time, and by experiencing all my emotions you've helped me to move forward.

Thank you for guiding me away from unhealthy coping strategies, as I've learned to navigate my emotions in healthier ways. The black hole of sadness that used to consume me has been filled with a golden light. I can accept that I will always miss Aura because I will always love her, and she will always be deceased. I've come to accept that she knows I loved her when I said goodbye, and understands that my decision to say goodbye was out of love.

Her ability to enjoy the simple things in life has made a lasting impact on my life. Finding peace in the sun's warmth on our patio was a source of comfort for her, and now it is for me as well. Gratitude is a life lesson that I get to keep, and my grief has forever transformed me for the better. My ongoing relationship with Aura has incited more space to love others—most importantly, to love myself.

I found peace in writing this book and in doing my own work. I can feel the warmth of sunlight again. I have a renewed sense of connection that goes beyond her physical presence. Such a healing gift! I can now offer brighter love to the current dogs in my life: Nilla, Hero, and Lemon, as well as my human family. I also feel more connected to those who have passed, including Aura, Banana, Kit, and Bailey. I will continue to bask in the sunshine.

With acceptance and hope,

Krista

Ashes in a Field

I later discovered that my parents decided to have Claire Place Veterinary Hospice arrange to bury Bailey's ashes. There is a natural field in the countryside, a cemetery specifically for pets. My husband offered to me that this is also Aura's final resting place. How could I not know this? I realized that when I declined Aura's ashes all those years ago, I had no idea what became of them. Not because I didn't care, but because I couldn't accept the reality of what was happening. All these years, the concept of Aura's ashes was renting space in my spaceship. And after many tears while writing this book, the concept that her ashes exist has slowly become a reality.

It has been months since Bailey has passed, and I wish I could tell you that I've visited this real-world meadow where dogs are finally pain-free. I don't know why I've hesitated. I suspect the fact that Aura died during the COVID-19 pandemic, alongside my other life chaos at the time, contributed to my complicated grief. Maybe just knowing her ashes physically exist is something I'm still accepting. Perhaps there is still part of me that believes that if I go, then she is really gone.

If you know me, you might be surprised to hear me share these internal struggles throughout this book. To many people, these inner thoughts seem silly, but I know you understand. I've now made plans to visit Bailey and Aura—soon.

Finding Meaning

The end goal of bereavement work is to find meaning in the life and death of a loved one, and to feel reconnected. Finding meaning in this context refers to having the capacity to access the legacy of love they left behind, and noticing our inner growth as a result. We may never know why their death occurred. We may never agree to the circumstances of their passing. What may feel like a senseless death at first, can be transformed into a sense of action and purpose. The end result may look like becoming an advocate, a philanthropist, or a writer, or it can simply be feeling a sense of joy and appreciation for the wonderful time we had with them.

To get there, we have to explore not only why their death happened, but also why it happened to us, and how we are different now because it happened—to us!

Our sense of self has been challenged, forcing us to question our worthiness and place in the world. We may have been grappling with low self-esteem and a loss of confidence to exert control over our motivations, behaviours, and environment. If we take a deep look around, we can see that we do have control in many areas—just not in the department of life and death.

Self-Care Moment: Circle of Love

This guided meditation provides a comforting space for you to connect through the sensation of loving energy. Take your time with this meditation, allowing yourself to fully experience the circle of love around you.

Listen to the guided meditation here:

In Review

I want to express gratitude for your willingness to delve into the complexities of grief with me. Writing this book has been a profound learning experience in my journey, and I hope it provides valuable insights and support for your journey.

Grief can make you feel like you're drowning in sorrow, as it reminds you of what was taken from you without your consent. The sadness you feel represents your system's attempts to keep your relationship with your dog as it used to be. Your attachment system is trying to remodel your inner relationship, and it slowly learns how to do it.

It's crucial to remember that grief, trauma, psychosis, and depression are distinct experiences. This book aimed to provide you with helpful tools, but it's equally important to tap into the expertise of therapists and bereavement groups who specialize in guiding individuals through grief.

Throughout this book, I've explored various activities and techniques which can help stabilize your system, offering you more resilience. The focus has been on the importance of self-exploration, self-care, physical activity, mental wellness, and external support.

Some key activities include practicing the Gratitude Rock, which encourages you to reflect on present moments, thereby shifting your focus and rewiring yourself toward accessing positive emotions.

Another is the Circle of Love meditation, where you can visualize yourself surrounded by beings of love and acceptance, fostering a sense of connection and healing.

Growing Pleasant Feelings and Tapping Into Love creates a temporary internal shift, accessing positive emotions and sensations. By somatically identifying joyous moments, and giving them a cue word or name, you can more easily access these feelings as a self-regulation tool when big waves of emotions come up. The incorporation of slow tapping further enhances the more helpful shift.

Deep breathing, and journalling with reflection are also common themes. Enjoying sunlight and improving vagal tone can have both psychological and biological benefits. Additionally, embracing acceptance and practicing self-forgiveness are crucial steps in progressing through grief.

Sadness and yearning reside at the core of grief. It's normal to experience a mix of emotions and waves of pain after loss, and there is no rule for when the waves have to stop feeling big. Your feelings will fluctuate, and you might find yourself experiencing sadness, anger, guilt, relief, peace, joy, or numbness at different times, or all at once.

I've emphasized the importance of feeling the range of emotions that you are experiencing, and surrounding yourself with a support network who will compassionately witness and validate your grief. This could be with someone close to you, a therapist, or a supportive community. Others can help us witness our grief and help us with self-compassion. By recognizing these emotions as a normal response to loss, you can begin to process your grief in a healthy way.

You may also find yourself realizing the full extent of your loss and its impact on your life multiple times. This is because the process of adapting to your new reality involves going through different phases of grief more than once. Even as the sadness begins to ease, the process of adjusting to life without your dog continues. It's normal for reminders of your loss to come up unexpectedly. As you assimilate to and accommodate for the changes in your life, you will land in a place of healing.

Memories serve as a connection between the past and the present, helping you to transition from the world as it was, to the world as it is now. They play a crucial role in reshaping your connection and absorbing your new reality, so it's important to honour the memories of your dog's life as much as possible. You can do this by talking about them with others, reminiscing, and continuing to include them. This can look like touching and holding onto your dog's belongings, continuing rituals such as going for walks, visiting places that are special to your dog, or imagining what your dog would say or think about a current situation. As well, displaying photos of them can be a reminder of your love, loss, and their legacy.

It's perfectly natural to maintain a healthy ongoing connection with your dog, and this will develop organically, even without consciously engaging in any specific practices. If your current capacity only allows for basic self-care, that's absolutely okay and important for your well-being. It's okay if you're unable to focus on anything beyond taking care of yourself right now. The intensity of your pain will gradually lessen with time and repetition, and healing will unfold at its own pace. I promise it is possible to come a time when you can think of your dog and authentically smile without feeling consumed by sadness and yearning.

Furthermore, we've explored the concept of After-Death Communication (ADC), normalizing the experience of communicating with deceased loved ones and highlighting potential therapeutic benefits. Whether through visual, auditory, tactile, or olfactory experiences, an ADC can offer comfort and reassurance to those who have experienced loss. Science is starting to understand how these experiences are helpful. Even if you haven't had this kind of experience, it doesn't mean you loved your dog any less, or that your dog isn't still connected with you in some way.

As you move forward, you may find yourself facing situations or events that trigger memories of your dog. These reminders can be both comforting and challenging, stirring up emotions that you thought were resolved. It's important to remember that this is a natural part of the grieving process and doesn't mean that you're regressing. Instead, it's an opportunity to acknowledge your feelings and continue the process of adapting to life without your dog by your side.

Know that your sadness and yearning are a testament to the impact your dog had on your life; you must allow yourself to feel whatever emotions come up. Journal, talk, dance, scream, cry, run, get therapy—just feel it fully!

If you are reading this book in anticipation of a loss, I'll assume you have the advantage of time to prepare. My suggestion is to lay down next to your dog on the floor, and tell them everything you want them to know before they leave this life. If you forget something, you can still share it after they are gone, but try to remember to let them know why you love them, why you'll miss them, and how you will remember them. Tell them why their life mattered, and how they have forever enriched your life. Maybe make a deal as to how you'll find each other in the afterlife, if that works within your beliefs.

Their Love & Legacy Shines on Within

The title of this book, *Over the Rainbow: The Love, Loss, and Legacy of Your Dog*, was chosen with deep empathy and understanding of the emotional journey you're navigating. Each aspect—love, loss, and legacy—is profoundly significant in honouring your journey and celebrating your special bond.

The profound sense of *loss* you're experiencing is a reflection of the bond and *love* you have with your beloved canine. You would not feel this type of loss if you had not first experienced a strong attachment and love. Your heartache is valid, and it's okay to feel the depth of your pain.

Your dog's *legacy* lives on in your heart and in your memories, shaping the way you navigate life without them physically here. Moving through your grief journey requires gentle acknowledgment of the permanence of your dog's passing, embracing the beautiful memories and lessons they left behind, and knowing that you have been forever changed for the better because of them.

Over the Rainbow was chosen as imagery and symbolization of the ongoing connection you have with your dog, transcending the limitations of the physical. While science may not be able to fully explain After-Death Communication yet, it is part of a profound connection that extends beyond the boundaries of time and space. Believing that you will one day be reunited can be very comforting.

You must move towards the storm and not just be next to it. Embracing your memories and strengthening your emotional connections with resilience is key.

You've learned that your grief is a story about love, and that under feelings of yearning, avoidance, numbness, and anger, lives sadness. You're grieving primary and secondary losses—what and who is gone. This includes the forced change in your current world, and lost opportunities in the future.

It's natural to long for your dog's companionship and wish they were still here. In fact, you will always wish your dog was here because you will always love them, and that's okay. Even after you're able to transform and let go of the pain, you will never forget your dog because the bond you share remains an integral part of who you are. Your connection continues.

What is your dog's legacy? They left you a gift, or else you would never have picked up this book. How did they show their love? Did they teach you that you are worthy of love? Were they able to break through your fortress and make you feel seen? Did they remind you to play and be present? You must find their kind and loving voice within you, because that is their message, and what you deserve.

The richness of our connections and shared experience with others is what forms the essence of life's meaningfulness. What a profound privilege to have experienced the love and companionship of a canine friend—a gift that shines within you forever.

ACKNOWLEDGEMENTS

A special recognition to all the dogs who have entered my life—those who have shared my home, those I've fostered, and those of friends, family members and clients. Thank you for providing me with meaning and inspiration.

To those who gifted your precious memories and photos of love and loss, your contribution honours your pet, and will bring healing for all who read it. To those who offered interviews, your time and expertise are greatly appreciated.

A heartfelt thank you to Kyle Poon for contributing the beautiful foreword to this book. Your words set a compassionate tone that honours the journey of love, loss, and legacy. Thank you for lending your voice to support all who read this book.

To my family, especially my husband Malcolm, thank you for your support and patience throughout the creation of this project. Without you, this would not have been possible.

Thank you to my writing coach, Kathy Sparrow, for your professional guidance and helping me take on the task of self-publishing. I value your wisdom and am grateful for your patience throughout this process!

A special shout-out to Trina Brunk for sharing your beautiful voice and musical talent to enrich the audio version of this book and guided meditations.

Finally, to my beta readers—your honest feedback and insight have challenged me to forge this labour of love into a book that, I hope, will support others navigating the loss of a cherished pet.

Together, we can continue spreading love, hope, and healing!
If this book has touched your heart or provided support, please consider sharing a testimonial to help others on their journey. Visit kristahelman.com to share how this book impacted you, a meaningful lesson, or a personal insight.

REFERENCES

Beder, Joan. "Loss of the Assumptive World—How We Deal with Death and Loss." *OMEGA - Journal of Death and Dying* 50, no. 4 (June 2005): 255–65. https://doi.org/10.2190/gxh6-8vy6-bq0r-gc04.

Beischel, J. Spontaneous, Facilitated, Assisted, and Requested After-Death Communication Experiences and their Impact on Grief. Accessed April 6, 2024. https://www.researchgate.net/publication/334330476_Spontaneous_Facilitated_Assisted_and_Requested_After-Death_Communication_Experiences_and_their_Impact_on_Grief_Peer-reviewed_referenced_commentary.

Bohlmeijer, Ernst T., Jannis T. Kraiss, Philip Watkins, and Marijke Schotanus-Dijkstra. "Promoting Gratitude as a Resource for Sustainable Mental Health: Results of a 3-Armed Randomized Controlled Trial up to 6 Months Follow-Up." *Journal of Happiness Studies* 22, no. 3 (May 7, 2020): 1011–32. https://doi.org/10.1007/s10902-020-00261-5.

Botkin, Allan L., and R. Craig Hogan. *Induced after-death communication: A miraculous therapy for grief and loss.* Charlottesville, VA: Hampton Roads, 2014.

Bretherton, Inge. "The Origins of Attachment Theory: John Bowlby and Mary Ainsworth." *A century of developmental psychology.*, 1994, 431–71. https://doi.org/10.1037/10155-029.

Claire Place Veterinary Hospice. "Do Pets Grieve?" Claire Place Veterinary Hospice Mobile Services, January 4, 2019. https://www.hospicevet.com/do-pets-grieve/.

Cotter, Prudence, Larissa Meysner, and Christopher William Lee. "Participant Experiences of Eye Movement Desensitization and Reprocessing vs. Cognitive Behavioural Therapy for Grief: Similarities and Differences." *European Journal of Psychotraumatology* 8, no. sup6 (October 9, 2017). https://doi.org/10.1080/20008198.2017.1375838.

Dent-Smyth, Kelly. "The Acute Stress Syndrome Stabilization Remote Individual (ASSYST-Ri) for Telemental Health Counseling after Adverse Experiences." *Psychology and Behavioral Science International Journal* 16, no. 2 (January 20, 2021). https://doi.org/10.19080/pbsij.2021.16.555932.

Elsaesser et al. "Investigation of the Phenomenology and Impact of Spontaneous and Direct After-Death Communications (ADCs): Research Findings." adcrp. Accessed April 6, 2024. https://www.adcrp.org/project.

Field, Nigel P., and Charles Filanosky. "Continuing Bonds, Risk Factors for Complicated Grief, and Adjustment to Bereavement." *Death Studies* 34, no. 1 (December 16, 2009): 1–29. https://doi.org/10.1080/07481180903372269.

Girianto, Pria Wahyu, Dhina Widayati, and Syahdila Sabrina Agusti. "Butterfly Hug to Reduce Anxiety on Elderly." *Jurnal Ners dan Kebidanan (Journal of Ners and Midwifery)* 8, no. 3 (December 26, 2021): 295–300. https://doi.org/10.26699/jnk.v8i3.art.p295-300.

Hall, Christopher. "Bereavement Theory: Recent Developments in Our Understanding of Grief and Bereavement." *Bereavement Care* 33, no. 1 (January 2, 2014): 7–12. https://doi.org/10.1080/02682621.2014.902610.

Hewson, Helen, Niall Galbraith, Claire Jones, and Gemma Heath. "The Impact of Continuing Bonds Following Bereavement: A Systemic Review." *Death Studies*, June 19, 2023, 1–14. https://doi.org/10.1080/07481187.2023.2223593.

Hoggan, Sarah. "Pet Loss Grief; the Pain Explained | Sarah Hoggan DVM | TEDxTemecula." YouTube, November 10, 2022. https://www.youtube.com/watch?v=TkJGhQANjZo&list=PLu8TmV21M5S-gaO8eIy6ytwHSajAcfDH7&index=3.

Hoggan, Sarah. "The Emotional Costs of Euthanasia | Sarah Hoggan DVM | TEDxTemecula." YouTube, October 25, 2019. https://www.youtube.com/watch?v=Jh-KKjIJHfk&list=PLu8TmV21M5S-gaO8eIy6ytwHSajAcfDH7&index=4.

Hornsveld, Hellen K., Frieda Landwehr, Willeke Stein, Margaretha P. Stomp, Monique A. Smeets, and Marcel A. van den Hout. "Emotionality of Loss-Related Memories Is Reduced After Recall Plus Eye Movements but Not After Recall Plus Music or Recall Only." *Journal of EMDR Practice and Research* 4, no. 3 (August 2010): 106–12. https://doi.org/10.1891/1933-3196.4.3.106.

The Hospice Support Fund. Complicated Grief. Accessed April 7, 2024. https://static1.squarespace.com/static/5fe278aec01e323d6cc0bc73/t/60f98fccaa32ea2fffbf31b5/1626968012585/complicated-grief-report.pdf.

Huberman, Andrew. "The Science & Process of Healing from Grief | Huberman Lab Podcast #74." YouTube, May 30, 2022. https://www.youtube.com/watch?v=dzOvi0Aa2FA.

James, John, and Russell Friedman. *The grief recovery handbook: The action program for moving beyond death, divorce, and other losses including health, career, and faith.* New York, NY: William Morrow, an imprint of HarperCollins Publishers, 2017.

Jarero, Ignacio, Lucina Artigas, and Marilyn Luber. "The EMDR Protocol for Recent Critical Incidents: Applications in a Disaster Mental Health Continuum of Care Context." *Journal of EMDR Practice and Research* 5, no. 3 (2011): 82–94. https://doi.org/10.1891/1933-3196.5.3.82.

Jarero, Ignacio. "Randomized Controlled Clinical Trial on the Provision of the EMDR-PRECI to Family Caregivers of Patients with Autism Spectrum Disorder." *Psychology and Behavioral Science International Journal* 11, no. 1 (March 19, 2019). https://doi.org/10.19080/pbsij.2019.11.555802.

Jarero, Ignatio. AIP Model-Based Acute Trauma and Ongoing Traumatic Stress Theoretical Conceptualization, 2022. https://www.researchgate.net/publication/322144707_AIP_model-based_Acute_Trauma_and_Ongoing_Traumatic_Stress_Theoretical_Conceptualization.

Jordan, John. "Guided Imaginal Conversations with the Deceased." Techniques of Grief Therapy, May 23, 2012, 282–85. https://doi.org/10.4324/9780203152683-86.

Kessler, David. Finding meaning: The sixth stage of grief. New York, NY: Scribner, 2020.

"Kidsgrief.Ca." Kids Grief. Accessed June 11, 2024. https://kidsgrief.ca/.

Kubler-Ross, Elisabeth. *On death and dying: What the dying have to teach doctors, nurses, clergy and their own families*. Scribner, 2014.

Luber, Marilyn. "Protocol for Excessive Grief." *Journal of EMDR Practice and Research* 6, no. 3 (2012): 129–35. https://doi.org/10.1891/1933-3196.6.3.129.

McCormick, B, and N Tassell-Matamua. "After-Death Communication: A Typology of Therapeutic Benefits." *Journal of Near-Death Studies* 34, no. 3 (2016). https://doi.org/10.17514/jnds-2016-34-3-p151-172.

McDonnell, F. EMDR and Bereavement, 2009. http://www.emdryorkshire.org/resource/FokkinaMcDonnell-Workshop5.pdf.

McInerny, Norma. "We Don't 'Move on' from Grief. We Move
        Forward with It | Nora McInerny | Ted." YouTube, April
        25, 2019. https://www.youtube.com/watch?v=khkJkR-
        ipfw&list=PLu8TmV21M5S-
        gaO8eIy6ytwHSajAcfDH7&index=2.

Mead, Nathaniel. "Benefits of Sunlight: A Bright Spot for Human
        Health." *Environmental Health Perspectives* 116, no. 4 (April
        2008). https://doi.org/10.1289/ehp.116-a160.

Menon, Sukanya B., and C. Jayan. "Eye Movement Desensitization and
        Reprocessing: A Conceptual Framework." *Indian Journal of
        Psychological Medicine* 32, no. 2 (July 2010): 136–40.
        https://doi.org/10.4103/0253-7176.78512.

Meysner, Larissa, Prudence Cotter, and Christopher W. Lee.
        "Evaluating the Efficacy of EMDR with Grieving
        Individuals: A Randomized Control Trial." *Journal of EMDR
        Practice and Research* 10, no. 1 (2016): 2–12.
        https://doi.org/10.1891/1933-3196.10.1.2.

Mol, Saskia S., Arnoud Arntz, Job F. Metsemakers, Geert-Jan Dinant,
        Pauline A. Vilters-van Montfort, and J. André Knottnerus.
        "Symptoms of Post-Traumatic Stress Disorder after Non-
        Traumatic Events: Evidence from an Open Population
        Study." *British Journal of Psychiatry* 186, no. 6 (June 2005):
        494–99. https://doi.org/10.1192/bjp.186.6.494.

Neimeyer, Robert. *New techniques of grief therapy: Bereavement and
        beyond.* New York: Routledge, 2022.

Nuwer, Rachel. "The 'rainbow Bridge' Has Comforted Millions of Pet
        Parents. Who Wrote It?" Animals, February 22, 2023.
        https://www.nationalgeographic.com/animals/article/rai
        nbow-bridge-poem-pet-death-mourning-origin-revealed.

O'Connor, Mary-Frances. "Mary Francis O'Connor: The Grieving
    Brain." YouTube, May 22, 2022.
    https://www.youtube.com/watch?v=nLh1F41RsM8.

O'Connor, Mary-Frances, David Wellisch, Annette Stanton, Naomi
    Eisenberger, Michael Irwin, and Matthew Lieberman.
    "Craving Love? Enduring Grief Activates Brain's Reward
    Center." *NeuroImage* 42, no. 2 (August 2008): 969–72.
    https://doi.org/10.1016/j.neuroimage.2008.04.256.

O'Connor, Mary-Frances, David Wellisch, Annette Stanton, Richard
    Olmstead, and Michael Irwin. "Diurnal Cortisol in
    Complicated and Non-Complicated Grief: Slope Differences
    across the Day." *Psychoneuroendocrinology* 37, no. 5 (May 2012):
    725–28. https://doi.org/10.1016/j.psyneuen.2011.08.009.

O'Connor, Mary-Frances, John Allen, and Alfred Kaszniak. "Emotional
    Disclosure for Whom?" *Biological Psychology*68, no. 2 (February
    2005): 135–46.
    https://doi.org/10.1016/j.biopsycho.2004.04.003.

O'Connor, Mary-Frances, Katherine Shear, Rachel Fox, Natalia
    Skritskaya, Bevin Campbell, Angela Ghesquiere, and Kim
    Glickman. "Catecholamine Predictors of Complicated Grief
    Treatment Outcomes." *International Journal of Psychophysiology*
    88, no. 3 (June 2013): 349–52.
    https://doi.org/10.1016/j.ijpsycho.2012.09.014.

O'Connor, Mary-Frances. *The Grieving Brain: The surprising science of
    how we learn from love and loss*. CA: HarperCollins Publishers,
    2023.

Parkes, Colin Murray. *Love and loss: The roots of grief and its
    complications*. London: Routledge, 2009.

Passoni, Serena, Teresa Curinga, Alessio Toraldo, Manuela Berlingeri, Isabel Fernandez, and Gabriella Bottini. "Eye Movement Desensitization and Reprocessing Integrative Group Treatment Protocol (EMDR-IGTP) Applied to Caregivers of Patients with Dementia." *Frontiers in Psychology* 9 (June 15, 2018). https://doi.org/10.3389/fpsyg.2018.00967.

Prigerson, Holly G., Paul A. Boelen, Jiehui Xu, Kirsten V. Smith, and Paul K. Maciejewski. "Validation of the New DSM-5-TR Criteria for Prolonged Grief Disorder and the PG-13-Revised (PG-13-R) Scale." *World Psychiatry* 20, no. 1 (January 12, 2021): 96–106. https://doi.org/10.1002/wps.20823.

Rando, Therese A. *How to go on Living when someone you love dies.* Lexington, MA.: Bantam Books, 1991.

Rando, Therese A. *Treatment of Complicated Mourning.* Champaign, IL: Research Press, 1995.

Rando, Therese A., Kenneth J. Doka, Stephen Fleming, Maria Helena Franco, Elizabeth A. Lobb, Colin Murray Parkes, and Rose Steele. "A Call to the Field: Complicated Grief in the DSM-5." *OMEGA - Journal of Death and Dying* 65, no. 4 (December 2012): 251–55. https://doi.org/10.2190/om.65.4.a.

Shapiro, Francine. *Eye movement desensitization and reprocessing (EMDR): Basic principles, protocols, and procedures.* 3rd ed. New York: Guilford Press, 2018.

Shapiro, Robin. *EMDR Solutions: Pathways to Healing.* New York: W.W. Norton, 2005.

Shapiro, Robin. "Visual Aids for Psychotherapy: Tools You Can Use," 2011.

Solomon, R.M., and T.A. Rando. "Treatment of Grief and Mourning through EMDR: Conceptual Considerations and Clinical Guidelines." *European Review of Applied Psychology* 62, no. 4 (October 2012): 231–39. https://doi.org/10.1016/j.erap.2012.09.002.

Solomon, Roger M., and Therese A. Rando. "Utilization of EMDR in the Treatment of Grief and Mourning." *Journal of EMDR Practice and Research* 1, no. 2 (October 2007): 109–17. https://doi.org/10.1891/1933-3196.1.2.109.

Solomon, Roger, and Barbara Hensley. "EMDR Therapy Treatment of Grief and Mourning in Times of Covid-19 (Coronavirus)." *Journal of EMDR Practice and Research* 14, no. 3 (July 29, 2020): 162–74. https://doi.org/10.1891/emdr-d-20-00031.

Solomon, Roger, and Francine Shapiro. "EMDR and the Adaptive Information Processing Modelpotential Mechanisms of Change." *Journal of EMDR Practice and Research* 2, no. 4 (November 2008): 315–25. https://doi.org/10.1891/1933-3196.2.4.315.

Sprang, Ginny. "The Use of Eye Movement Desensitization and Reprocessing (EMDR) in the Treatment of Traumatic Stress and Complicated Mourning: Psychological and Behavioral Outcomes." *Research on Social Work Practice* 11, no. 3 (May 2001): 300–320. https://doi.org/10.1177/104973150101100302.

Titcombe, Lianna. "When a Beloved Pet Dies: The Best and Worst Things to Say to People in Grief." Canadian Animal Shelter & Community Medicine Association, July 21, 2022. https://www.cascma.org/when-a-beloved-pet-dies/.

Unanue, Wenceslao, Marcos Esteban Gomez Mella, Diego Alejandro Cortez, Diego Bravo, Claudio Araya-Véliz, Jesús Unanue, and Anja Van Den Broeck. "The Reciprocal Relationship between Gratitude and Life Satisfaction: Evidence from Two Longitudinal Field Studies." *Frontiers in Psychology* 10 (November 8, 2019). https://doi.org/10.3389/fpsyg.2019.02480.

"What Is Grief?" What is Grief? Accessed April 6, 2024. https://www.mayoclinic.org/patient-visitor-guide/support-groups/what-is-grief.

Walker, Matthew P. *Why we sleep: Unlocking the power of sleep and dreams*. New York, NY: Scribner, an imprint of Simon & Schuster, Inc, 2018.

Williamson, Chris. "Control Your Mind for Extreme Motivation and Focus - Andrew Huberman." YouTube, July 7, 2022. https://www.youtube.com/watch?v=31DMZLK_PPs&t=2261 s.

Wojtkowiak, Joanna, Jonna Lind, and Geert Smid. "Ritual in Therapy for Prolonged Grief: A Scoping Review of Ritual Elements in Evidence-Informed Grief Interventions." *Frontiers in Psychiatry* 11 (February 3, 2021). https://doi.org/10.3389/fpsyt.2020.623835.

Wong, Joel., Jesse Owen, Nicole Gabana, Joshua Brown, Sydney McInnis, Paul Toth, and Lynn Gilman. "Does Gratitude Writing Improve the Mental Health of Psychotherapy Clients? Evidence from a Randomized Controlled Trial." *Psychotherapy Research* 28, no. 2 (May 3, 2016): 192–202. https://doi.org/10.1080/10503307.2016.1169332.

Worden, William. *Grief counselling and grief therapy: A handbook for the mental health practitioner*. 5th ed. Springer Publishing Company, LLC, 2018

ABOUT THE AUTHOR

Krista Helman is a compassionate therapist, author, and social worker based in Canada. With years of clinical experience, she is the founder and Director of the Trauma & Grief Institute (TGI), where she leads a team offering therapy, training, and community-based healing grounded in evidence-based and holistic practices.

She is the developer of the EMDR-GRIEF protocol, an integrative approach to processing grief using EMDR therapy, and she provides training for clinicians internationally. A sought-after speaker and presenter, Krista offers professional workshops, online courses, and transformative retreats for both the public and mental health professionals.

Krista is the author of *Over the Rainbow: The Love, Loss, and Legacy of Your Dog*, a heartfelt guide blending therapeutic strategies, psychoeducation, and personal stories for those mourning the loss of a beloved pet. She has also published *Self-Care Moments: A Workbook to Navigate Your Grief*.

While her expertise spans a wide range of therapeutic areas, Krista is particularly passionate about grief, trauma, and the human search for meaning. She has a deep interest in the phenomenon of after-death communication (ADC) and is committed to destigmatizing scientifically supported experiences that are often misunderstood.

When not working, Krista enjoys spending time with her family—both human and furry—and finds peace in the healing rhythms of nature.

KEYNOTES & WORKSHOPS

Krista would be pleased to receive your invitation to speak or present at your event. Her engaging presentations and interactive workshops offer accessible insights and practical strategies rooted in the latest mental health practices.

As the Director of the Trauma & Grief Institute (TGI) and the developer of the EMDR-GRIEF protocol, Krista leads a variety of workshops, classes, and training opportunities for both the public and clinicians. These offerings span a wide range of topics, from trauma and grief-specific content to general wellness, emotional resilience, and mind-body integration.

Krista presents at professional conferences and is particularly passionate about engaging with diverse audiences, including healthcare and veterinary professionals, workplace teams seeking a healthier culture, caregivers and frontline workers facing burnout, and organizations seeking impactful education on grief, trauma, and wellness.

She also holds a special interest in the phenomenon of after-death communication (ADC) and is committed to destigmatizing scientifically supported human experiences that remain poorly understood. Her offerings continue to evolve alongside her leadership at TGI, with a focus on compassion, connection, and evidence-based care.

Below you will find testimonials from individuals who have first-hand experience collaborating with Krista:

"Krista is a phenomenal presenter. She speaks from a perspective of someone who understands intimately her topics and not just from a theoretical perspective. She makes topics easy to understand and then apply in practice. She is knowledgeable, approachable and an enjoyable presenter to listen to."
—Julie Marquis, RP

"Krista is engaging and impactful. Even as a seasoned therapist I learned a lot from her well-researched presentation."
—Alison Sharp, RSW, LCSW

"Krista's presentations are well-researched and organized. She is clear, personable, and engaging. She integrates theory into practice with plenty of examples, videos, and opportunities for learners to practice the skills discussed. I have learned a lot from Krista and value her knowledge regarding EMDR, parts work, and grief counselling."
—Emily Davison, MSW, RSW

For more information, you can contact Krista at:
www.kristahelman.com

9 781068 846342